Rubber Pencil Devil
by
Alex Da Corte

Alex Da Corte:
An Alchemy of Images
by
Jamillah James

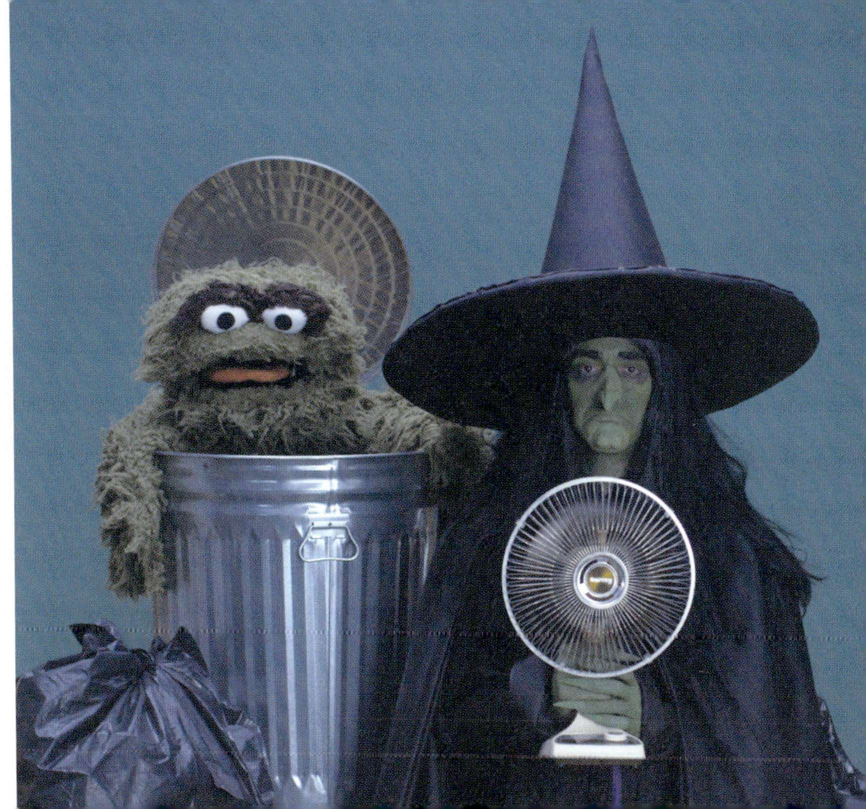

I believe I am in Hell,
therefore I am.

—Arthur Rimbaud,
<u>Night in Hell</u>

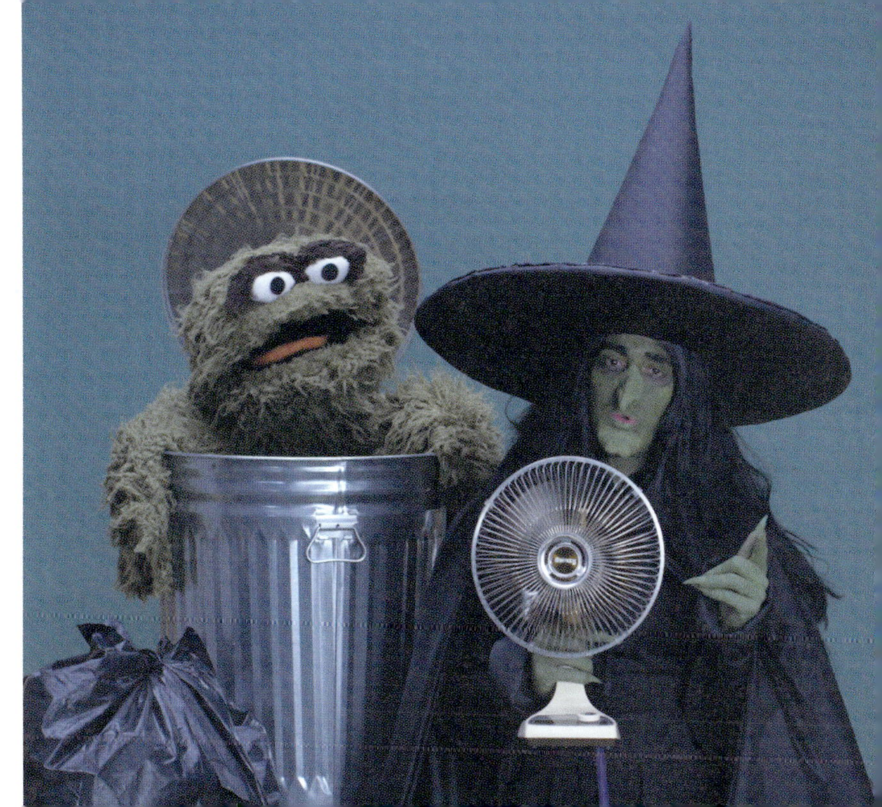

A Season in He'll is the first solo exhibition in Los Angeles devoted to the work of the Philadelphia-based interdisciplinary artist Alex Da Corte (b. 1980, Camden, NJ). The three-part site-specific installation, featuring new works and four recent videos never before presented together in the United States, continues the artist's years-long meditation on the French writer Arthur Rimbaud's long-form prose poem *A Season in Hell* (1873), which recounts the author's imagined descent into purgatory and his struggle with spiritual and emotional turmoil. Rimbaud wrote the poem shortly after ending his tumultuous affair with fellow Symbolist poet Paul Verlaine. Replete with dense imagery and linguistic flourishes yet scathing in its allegorical depiction of a romance in decline, the text can be taken as a metaphor for embattled queer identity and the path to self-actualization. Da Corte is interested in Rimbaud's exploration of interpersonal dynamics and their effect on identity and psychic formation, and he uses the poem as a framework to consider the role of spectacle and simulation in visual and popular culture.

Da Corte's videos, sculptures, paintings, and installations ruminate on personal and cultural politics, alienation, and the com-

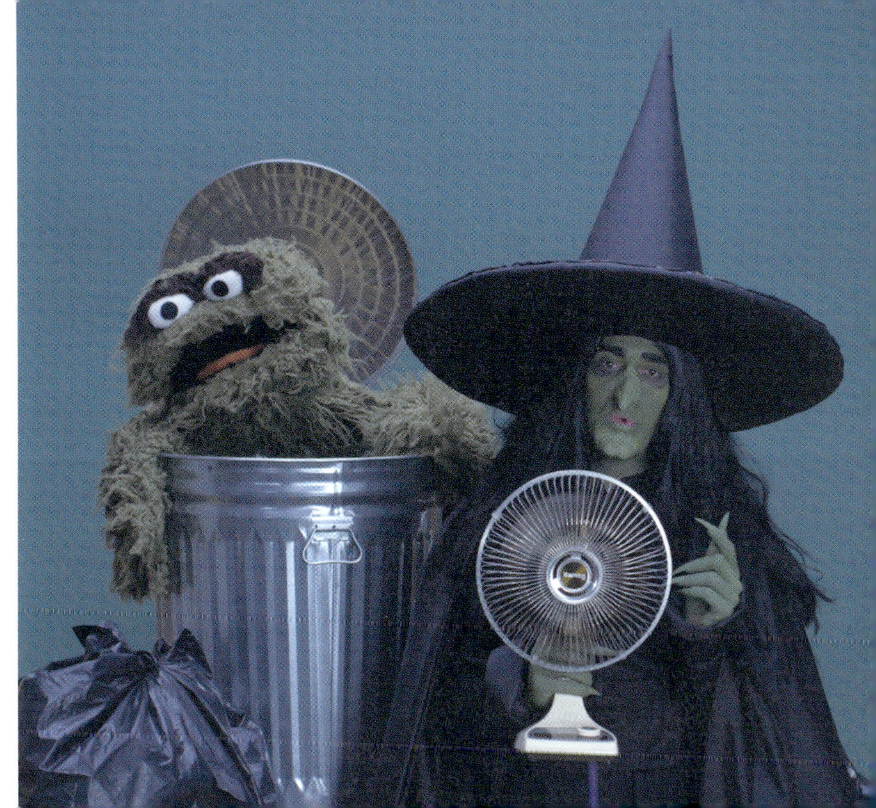

plexities of the human experience. Noted for his pop-informed sensibility and embrace of theatricality, he creates fantastical immersive environments that showcase his maximal surrealist impulses. Banal objects and consumer goods serve as both actors and props in his dreamy yet simultaneously nightmarish landscapes. The work encourages both free association and dissociation, the latter sensation an apt description of the state of mind of Rimbaud's protagonist until the poem's last chapter, "Farewell." There, after his figurative and emotional journey, he states, "my great advantage is that I can laugh at old love affairs full of falsehood, and stamp with shame such deceitful couples; I went through women's Hell over there—and I will be able now to possess the truth within one body and soul."[1] Rimbaud's dissociation is rendered in a few different ways: as a psychologically and existentially fractured state; as a break with reality, in the form of a delusional journey to hell; as an "othering" of his identity—as a woman, as a wretch, and, in a particularly caustic passage, as other races, described in pejorative terms;[2] and as a rejection of propriety about one's emotions and personal affairs. Rimbaud is incredibly candid about the nature of his

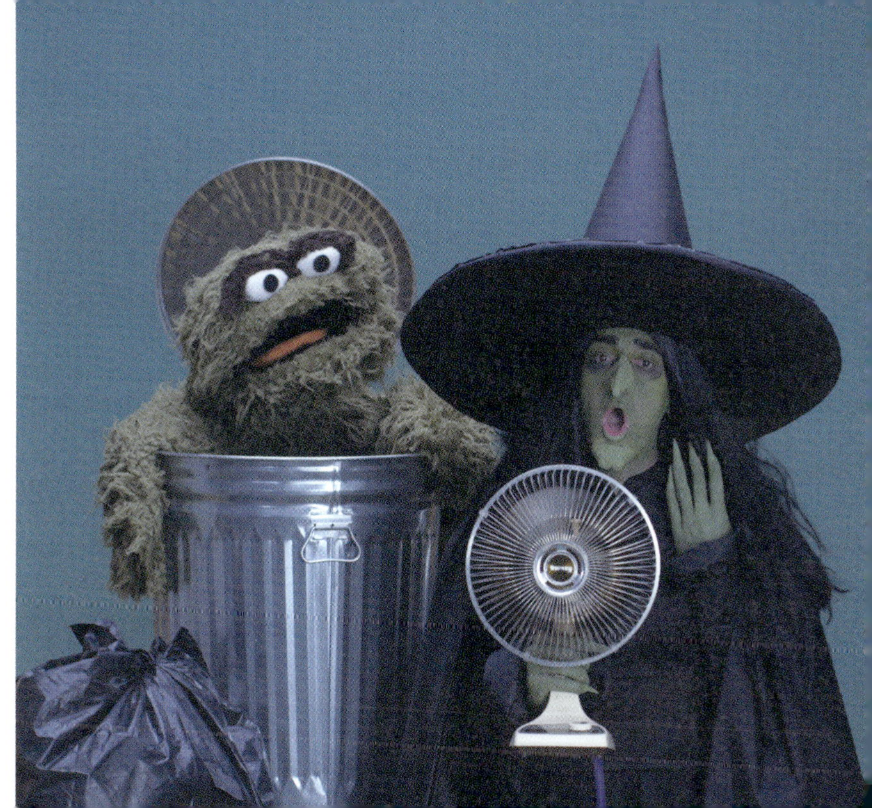

queer relationship, displaying an emotionality perhaps not typically expected of men:

> *I lived in his soul as if it were a palace that had been cleared out so that the most unworthy person in it would be you, that's all. Ah, really, I used to depend on him terribly ... And so my heartaches kept growing and growing, and I saw myself going more and more to pieces (and everyone else would have seen it, too, if I hadn't been so miserable that no one even looked at me anymore!) and still more and more I craved his affection ... His kisses and his friendly arms around me were just like heaven—a dark heaven, that I could go into, and where I wanted only to be left—poor, deaf, dumb, and blind ... I could feel myself with him gone, dizzy with fear, sinking down into the most horrible blackness—into death.*[3]

A Season in Hell demonstrates the paradox of "cruel optimism," or "the condition of maintaining an attachment to a problematic object" that is "discovered either to be impossible, sheer fantasy, or too possible, and toxic."[4] Rimbaud's vacillation between vulnerability and rage, reality and fantasy, positions

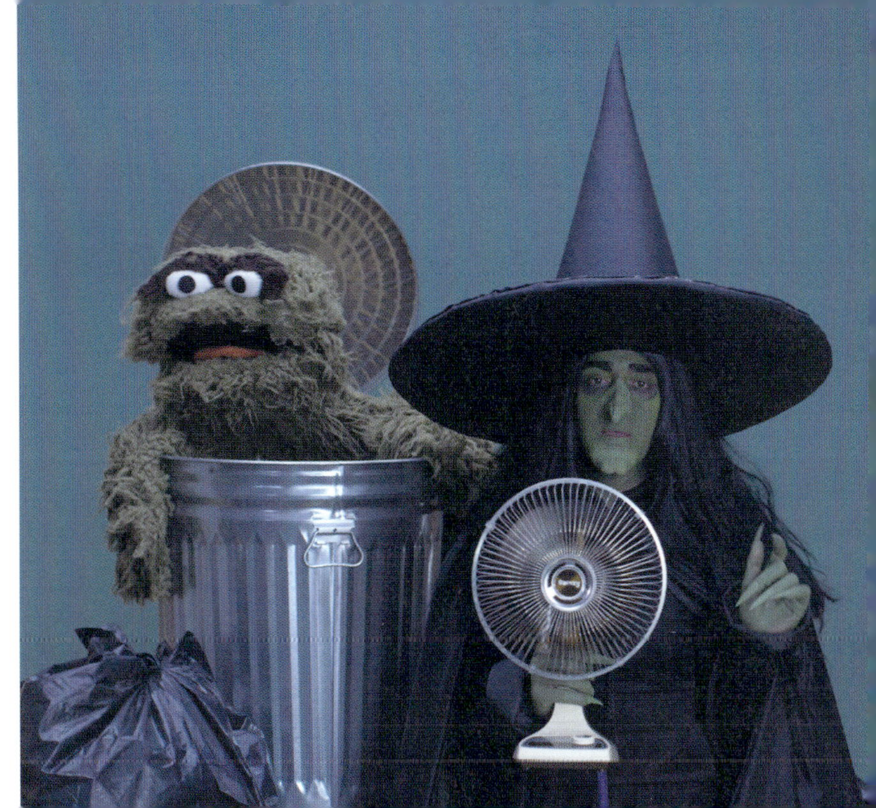

him as an unstable subject whose attachment to the object of his affection threatens his very being and constitution. Romanticizing the impossible at all costs challenges the persistence of reality, the future, and indeed the possible.

Similarly, Da Corte's work has a pervasive sense of instability and a sideways engagement with reality. This is manifested most directly in his videos; the moving image relies greatly on the viewer's suspension of disbelief or the ability to abandon preconceived notions of the "real world" and embrace an alternative reality in which anything is possible. Take, for instance, the centerpiece of the exhibition, a 2012 trilogy of videos titled after sections of Rimbaud's poem: A Season in Hell, Bad Blood, and The Impossible. Each video features an actor who bears a striking resemblance to the artist performing a series of ritualistic, mysterious, and occasionally violent gestures with a tableau of props. Set against a bright monochromatic backgrounds and accompanied by distinctive sound tracks, the videos become the space for Da Corte to trouble the performance of masculinity by testing the physical limits of his doppelgänger (the actor) as he follows

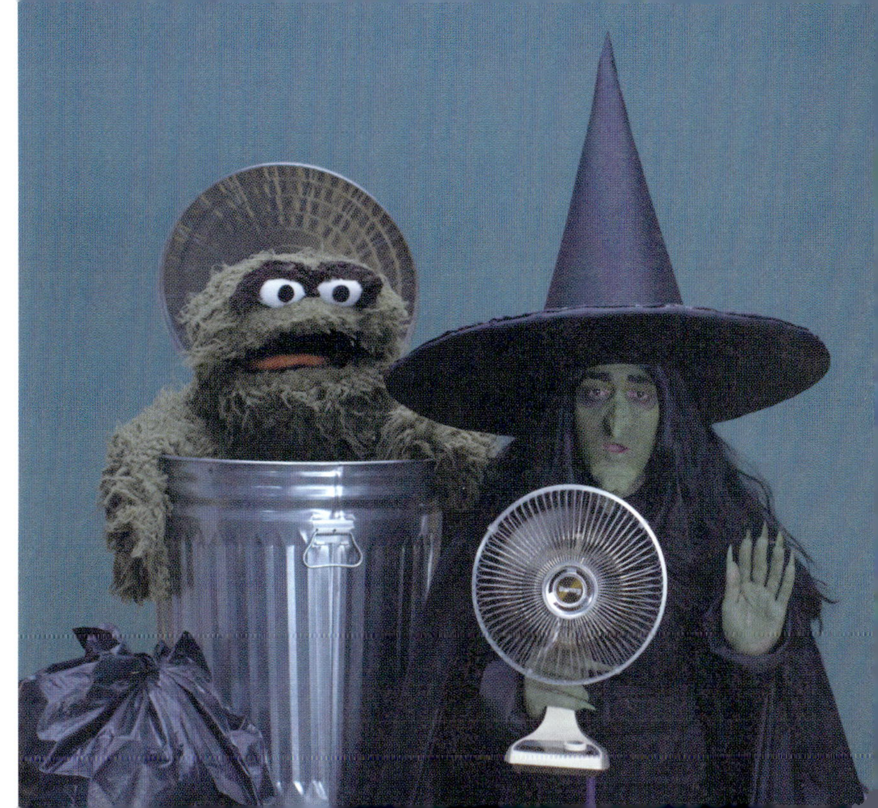

increasingly dangerous and challenging direction. Each video's protracted action registers as surreal, unreal; its slowness, coupled with the eeriness of the sound tracks, makes it seem more like a dream than a carefully constructed filmic reality. This dynamic culminates in A Night in Hell, Part II (2014), a hypnotic slow-motion video for which Da Corte hired a Hollywood stunt double to dress as a mummy and fall from an unknown height in front of a theatrical backdrop while on fire. Obscuring the identity of the actor encourages viewer identification, while the duration of the video's central action tests the viewer's capacity to accept its willful distortion of time and reality.

For this exhibition Da Corte has produced several new works, including a stained-glass window, chain-link curtains, and an over-size witch hat, inspired by a vari-ety of sources, including the Disney films Fantasia (1940) and Beauty and the Beast (1991) and the horror films of the Italian directors Dario Argento and Lamberto Bava.[5] This conflation of disparate sources further underscores the discursive and unstable nature of Da Corte's work. In these films, fantasy, magic, and the supernatural play significant roles

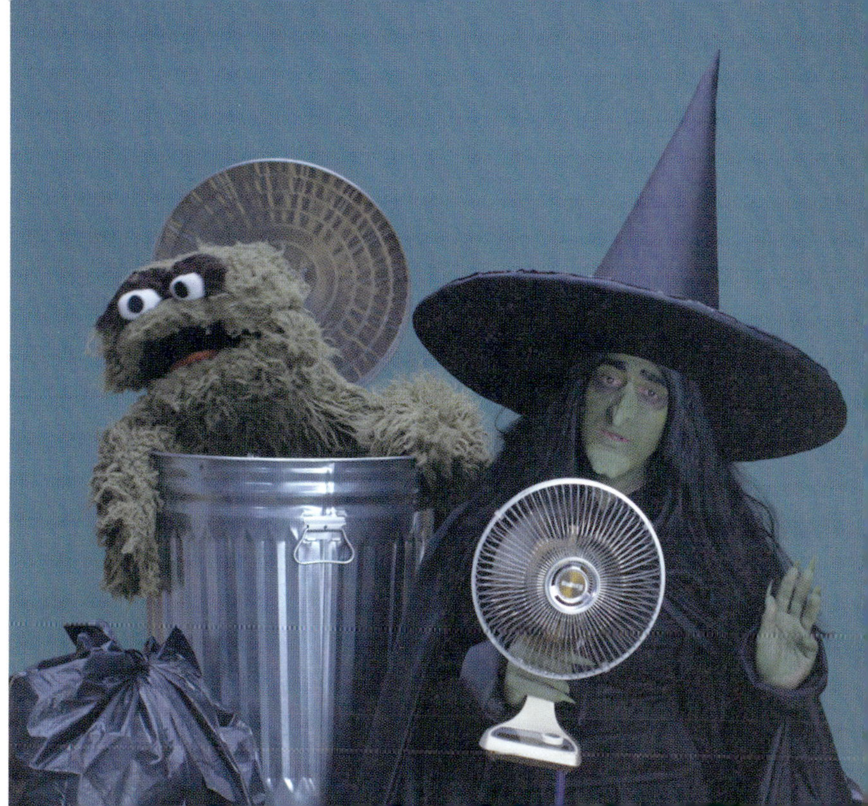

in existential battles between good and evil. Evil is often represented by witches, who employ tricks to best the story's hero. Yet these characters generally have a foil who is their alter ego in the service of good. The historical, literary, and cinematic depictions of witches fascinate Da Corte. He suggests that they are an inherently queer archetype representing human duality and isolation, serving to remind us of societal pressures to maintain decorum and control unsanctioned impulses. He has performed as a witch before, most notably in his videos *Easternsports* and *The Old Fart* (both 2014) and a series of photographs; it should be noted that he prefers the feminine witch to the masculine warlock, so inhabiting the role requires performance in drag. Witches embody a spirit of resistance and alienation, subject positions embraced in the recent work of scholars such as Sara Ahmed and Lee Edelman, who are associated with the so-called negative turn in queer theory. Edelman embraces alienation and the impossibility of a fully realized queer subject, whereas Ahmed posits a space for queerness to be "expressed as an embodiment of the freedom to be unhappy," running counter to what is commonly understood

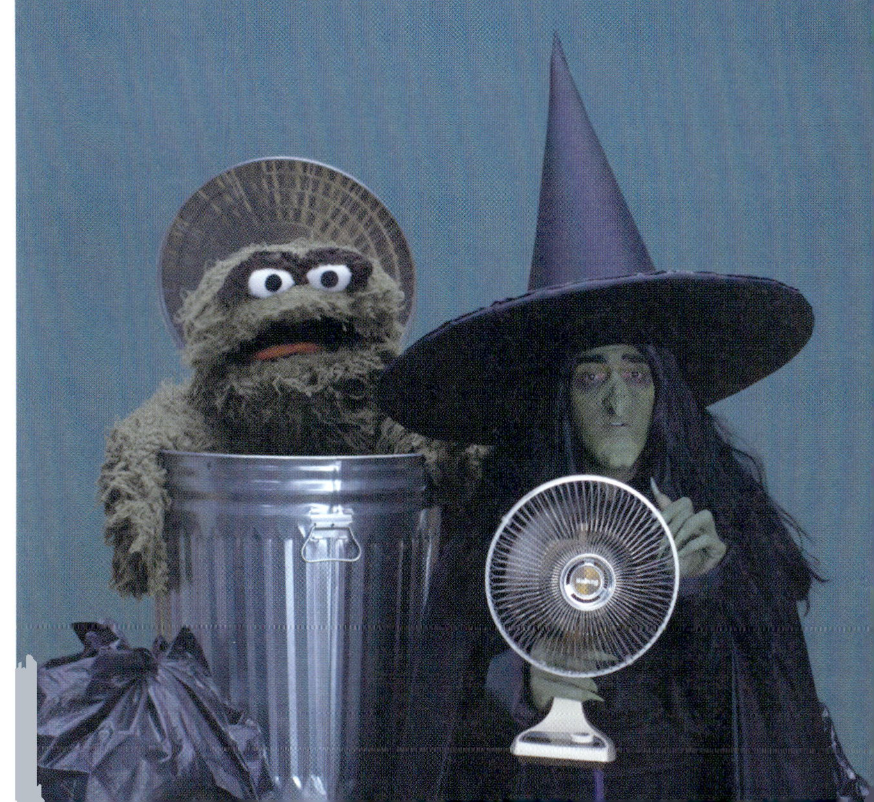

as "good" or "right"—that is, love, beauty, power, faith, happiness—to allow for a spectrum of queer feeling and being that is full and complex and not beholden to binary constructions.[6] Even in mainstream culture, there have been attempts to recode the cultural understanding of witches as not essentially evil but flawed or misunderstood, such as the novel and musical Wicked: The Untold Story of the Witches of Oz, a recast of The Wizard of Oz partly from the perspective of the Wicked Witch of the West. What is important in all these instances, and particularly in Da Corte's practice, is the insistence on a spectrum of possibilities between and outside of the binaries of good and evil, reality and fantasy, beauty and profanity. Witches (and the witch hat as signifier) become metonyms for the complex human experiences and aesthetic traditions addressed in his work.

Like Rimbaud, who found beauty "bitter—and insulted her," Da Corte constantly challenges the function of beauty in aesthetic production.[7] The rose, an enduring symbol of beauty and a recurring motif in Da Corte's work, makes an appearance here, as the central element of the stained-glass window. The image is appropriated from the

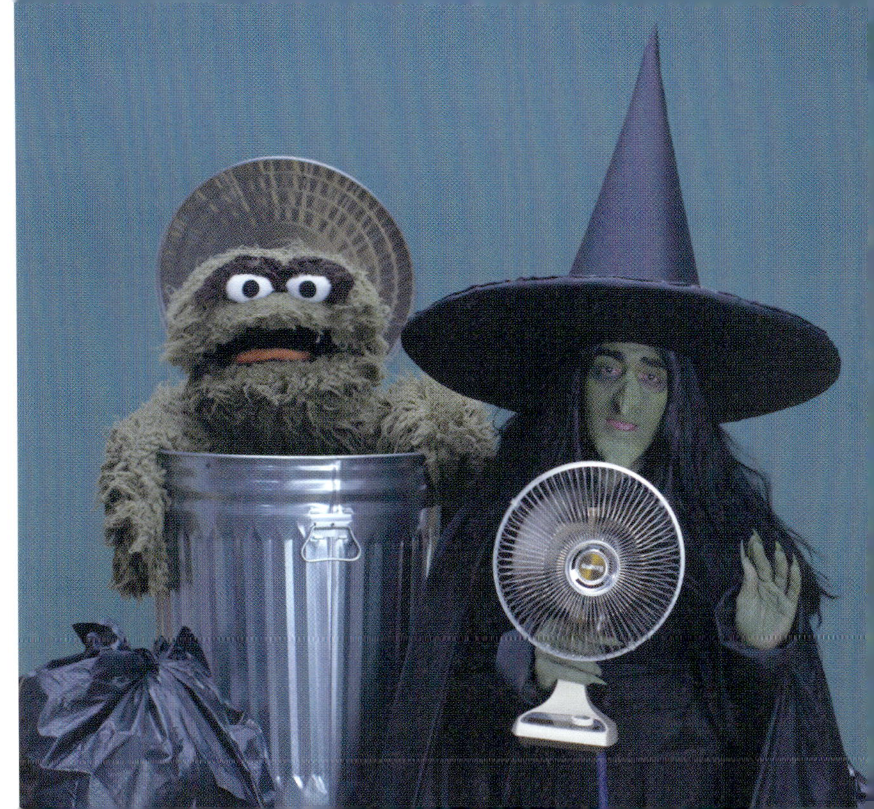

opening sequence of Disney's Beauty and the Beast, the rose a beautiful yet cruel reminder of the spell cast by a witch on a vain prince. Beauty is revealed as illusory and subjective. The rose is a signpost for territory less traveled, the outer limits of artistic beauty, which is where Da Corte's work falls, alongside that of his post-pop forebears the Los Angeles artists Mike Kelley and Paul McCarthy, whose work has privileged abjection, dark comedy, the grotesque, and failure.

Da Corte's installations transform a space entirely from floor to ceiling, using unconstrained aestheticism and ecstatic for-malism, as opposed to more controlled visual sensibilities. The colors are saturated, the flooring and seating ornamental, and the objects therein stylized—even the smell of a room is altered (with aromatic diffusers). The scene is rich with drama and intent. Elements of the carnivalesque are on display, referring to elaborate celebrations held through-out the world, such as carnival in parts of Latin America and Mardi Gras in New Orleans.[8] Da Corte is of Latino descent, and as a child he lived in Venezuela, where carnival is celebrated in the spring. As a public spectacle carnival allows its attendees to create a real-life world of fantasy and decadence

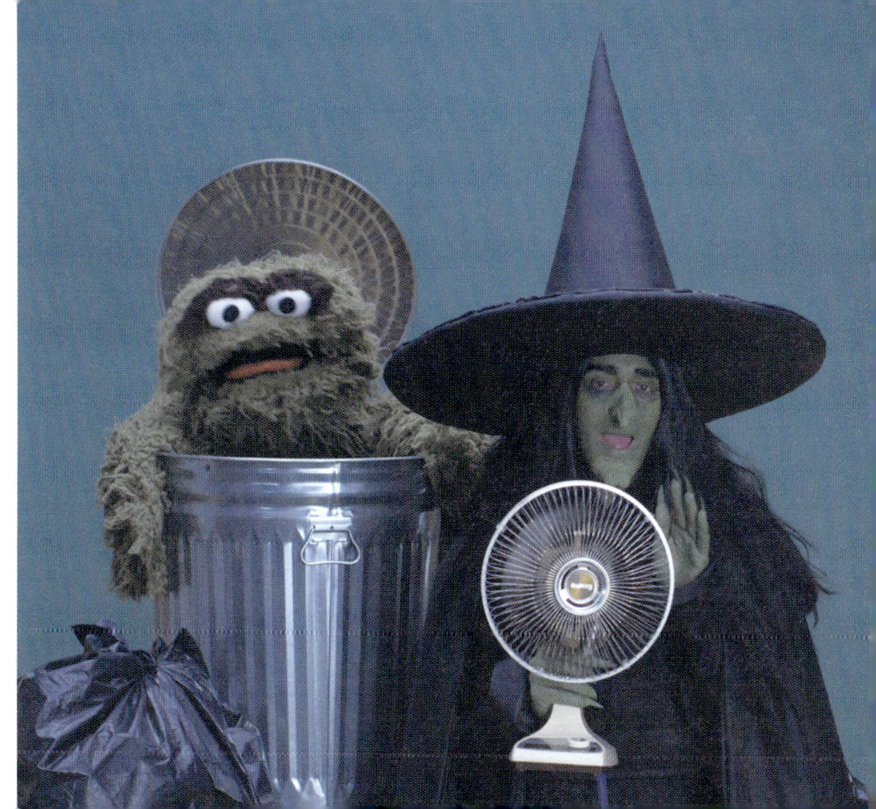

in which costumes and masks conceal identities and the senses are delighted and overwhelmed. Similarly, to enter into an exhibition of Da Corte's work is to encounter an alternative reality in which excess is a virtue and beauty and art historical precedent are under intense scrutiny.

A Season in He'll, in all its playfulness, also manifests a particular sense of unease. For one, the title is intentionally confusing. Da Corte chose to change the word hell to he'll, the contraction of "he will," to suggest a forward momentum, an ongoing quest, or instability in a subject's constitution, a concept that is central to Rimbaud's poem. Da Corte uses the witch and rose signifiers to connote a queer horizon that is concerned with the space between binaries, what is considered unfixed or unstable. Magic and illusion are central to Da Corte's work and are themselves queer technologies in the service of resistance. As Arthur Evans has observed, "By tapping into magic ... we are in league with the memories of the forest and our own forgotten faery selves, now banished to the underworld. Let us invoke our friends, the banished and forbidden spirits of nature and self, as well as the ghosts of Indian, wise-woman, faggot,

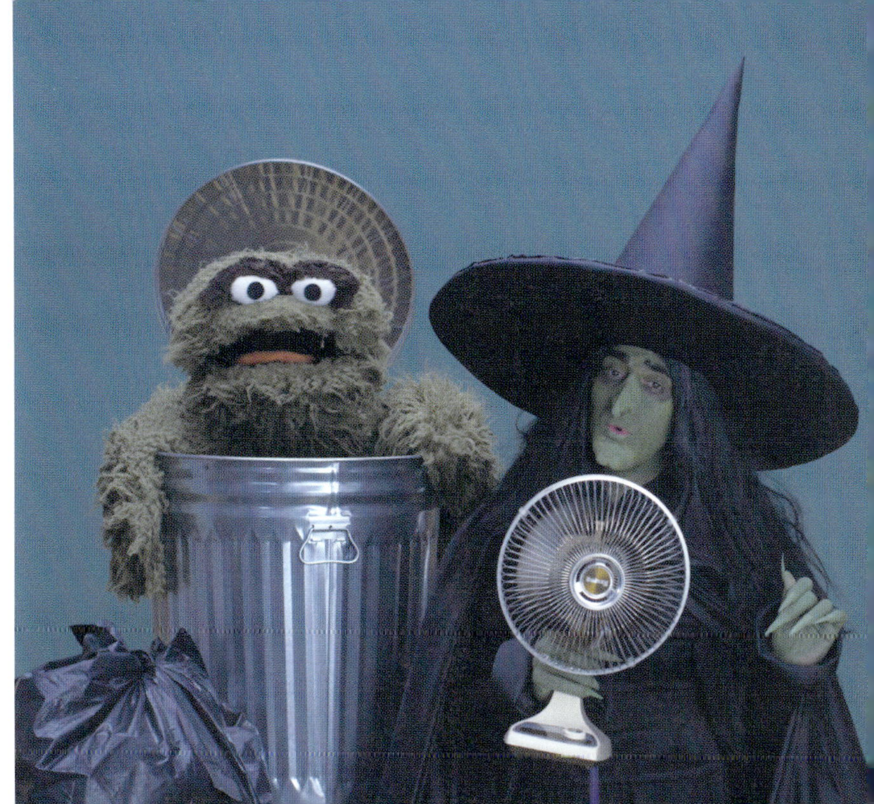

black sorcerer, and witch. They will hear our deepest call and come. Through us the spirits will speak again. A genuine counter-culture that affirms the magic of human life is an ominous threat to the entire industrial order."[9]

The realities that Da Corte constructs within his installations allow for a multiplicity of responses and interpretations. The exhibition is a symbolic rebus that places seemingly disparate objects in relation to one another; scale, texture, sensation, and humor heighten the experience. An archival family photograph from a joyous occasion assumes a sinister feel when taken out of context, the pattern of the exhibition's flooring forms a dizzying optical illusion that tests the surety of what lies underfoot, the speed of the videos on view defies an ordinary sense of time, and a witch hat is scaled to unexpected, absurdist proportions, invoking the uncanny. What seems impossible becomes possible. Fusing influences and images and reimagining the tropes that have animated the course of art history and cultural production, Da Corte uses the space of his work to perform a type of visual alchemy that conjures new aesthetic and political possibilities.

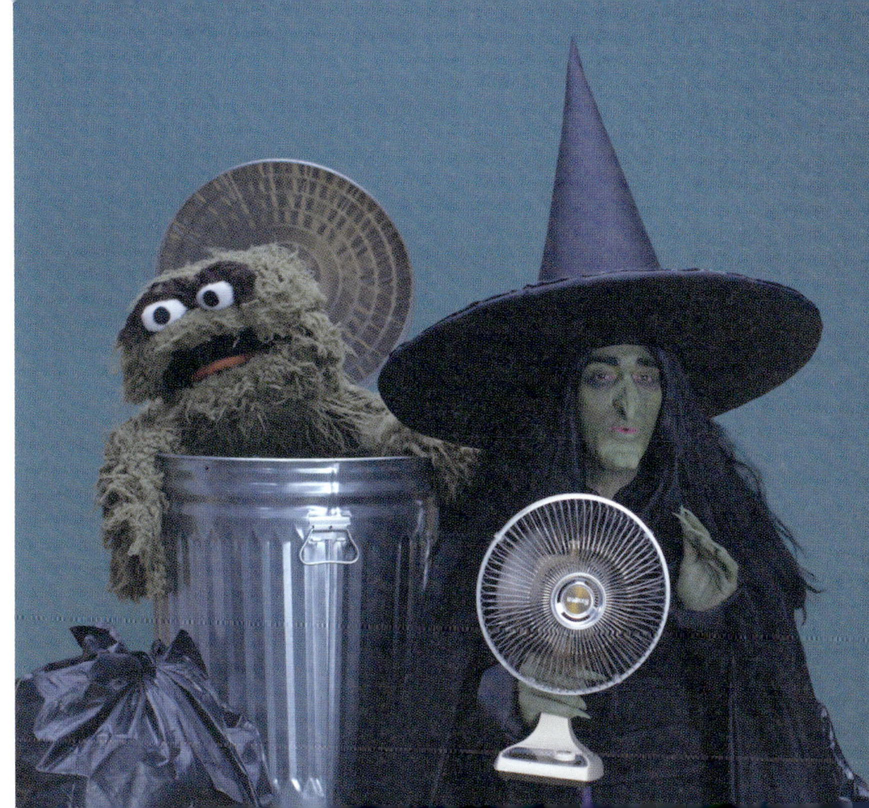

Notes

The title of this essay paraphrases that of a chapter in Arthur Rimbaud's A Season in Hell (1873), "Second Delirium: The Alchemy of the Word," in which he writes, in reference to his work as a poet: "The worn-out ideas of old-fashioned poetry played an important part in my alchemy of the word.... I explained my magical sophistries by turning words into visions!" A Season in Hell, in Arthur Rimbaud: Complete Works, trans. Paul Schmidt (New York: Harper Perennial, 2008), 232–38. Epigraph: Ibid., 225.

1 Ibid., 243
2 Rimbaud liberally uses a specific epithet referring to black people, commonplace at the time though generally understood as unacceptable by today's standards.
3 Rimbaud, A Season in Hell, 230
4 Lauren Berlant, "Cruel Optimism: On Marx, Loss, and the Senses," in "Happiness," ed. Sara Ahmed, special issue, New Formations, no. 63 (Winter 2007–8): 33.
5 See Argento's Three Mothers trilogy of films about witches holding dominion in three international cities—Suspiria (1977), Inferno (1980), and The Mother of Tears (2007)—and Bava's Demons (1985) and Demons II (1986), both cowritten by Argento.
6 Sara Ahmed, "Happiness and Queer Politics," World Picture Journal, 3 (Summer 2009): 15.
7 Rimbaud, A Season in Hell, 219.
8 The curator and scholar Claire Tancons has written extensively on the

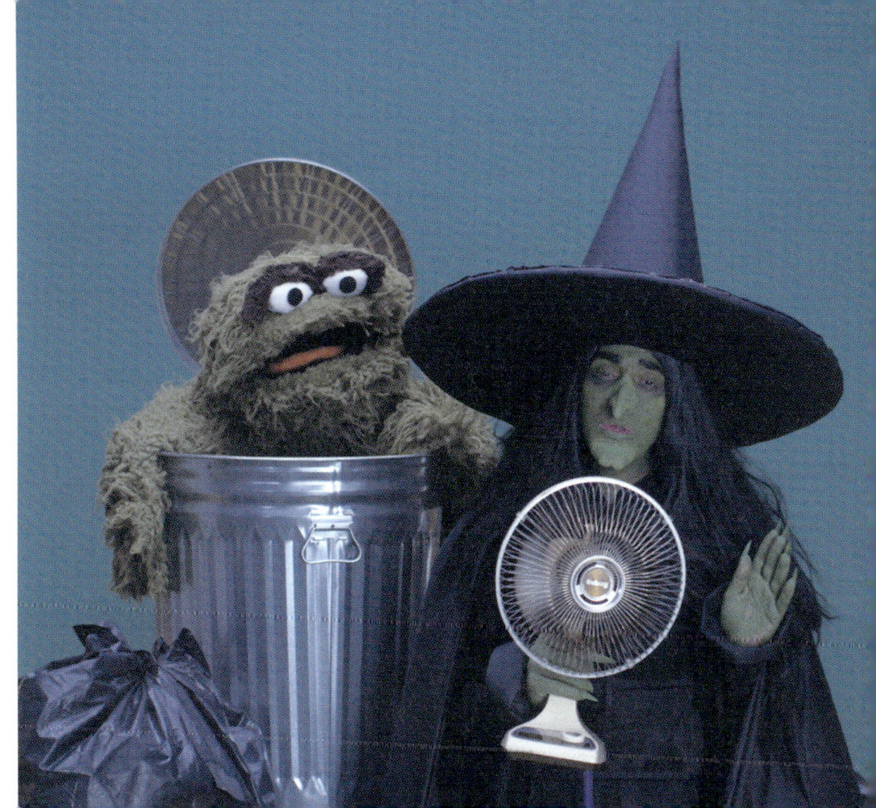

carnivalesque in the public sphere; see, for example, Claire Tancons and Jesse McKee, "On Carnival and Contractual Curating," Fillip, no. 13 (Spring 2011): 74–79. See more at clairetancons.com.

9 Arthur Evans, Witchcraft and the Gay Counterculture: A Radical View of Western Civilization and Some of the People It Has Tried to Destroy (Boston: Fag Rag Books, 1978), 173.

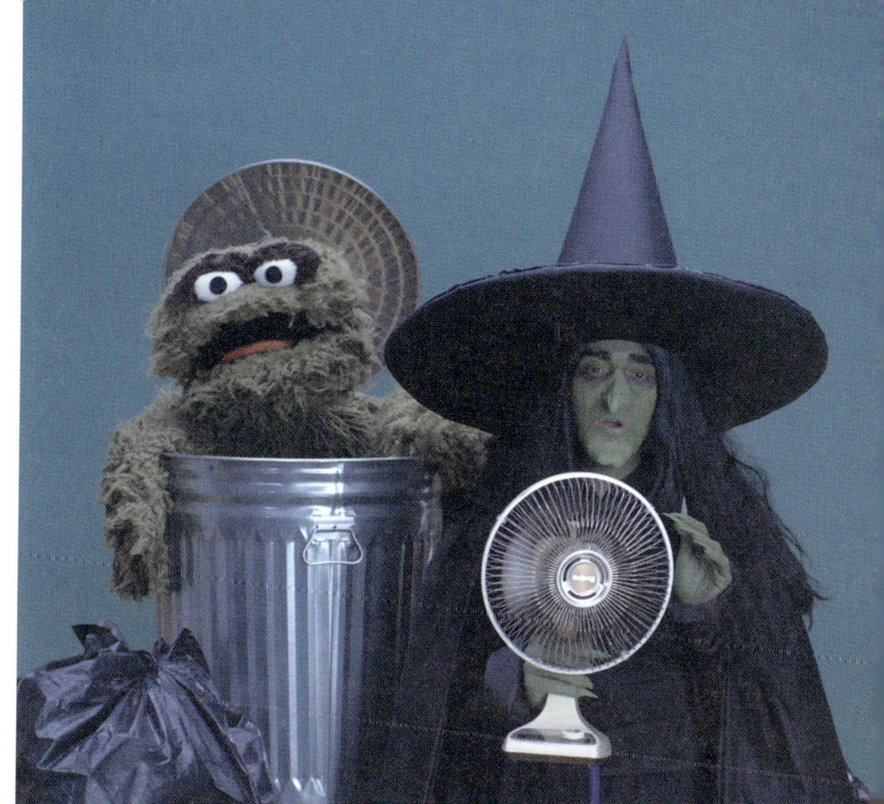

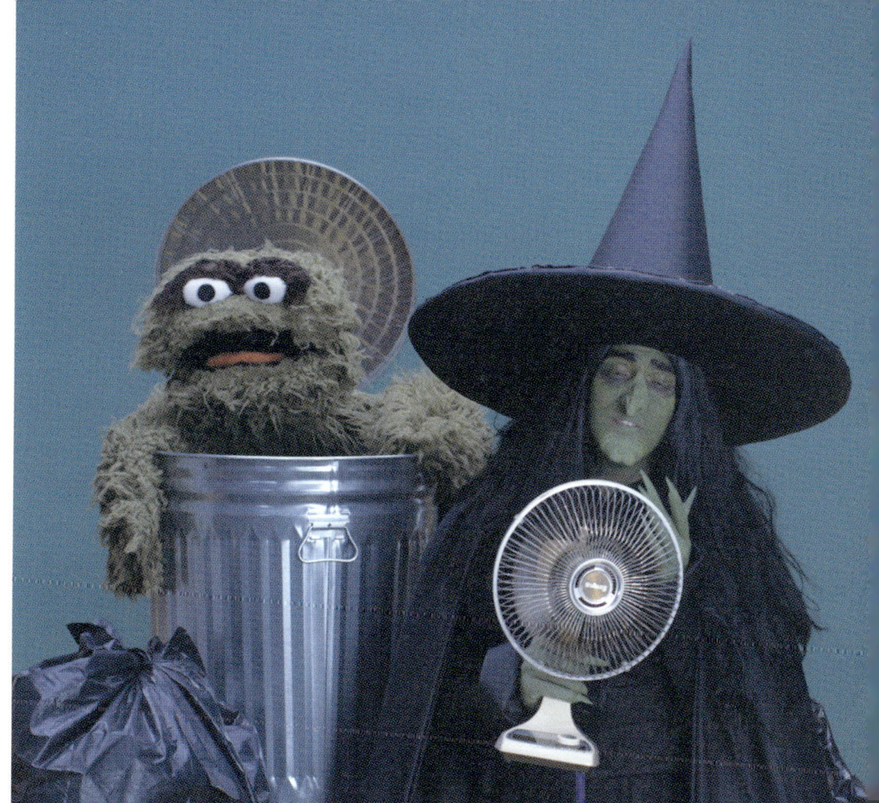

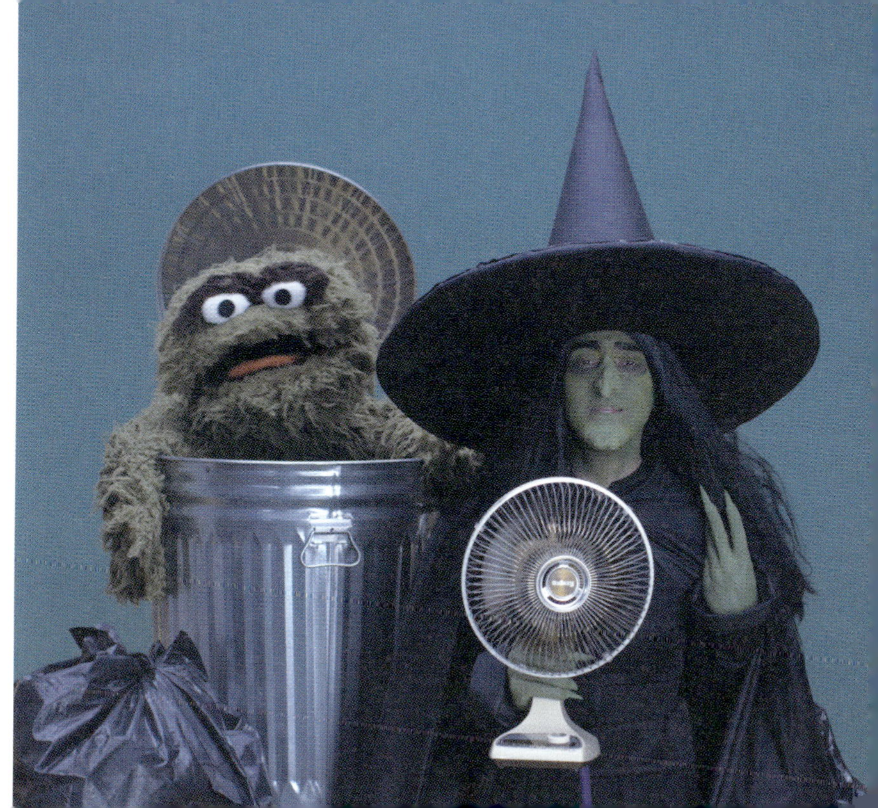

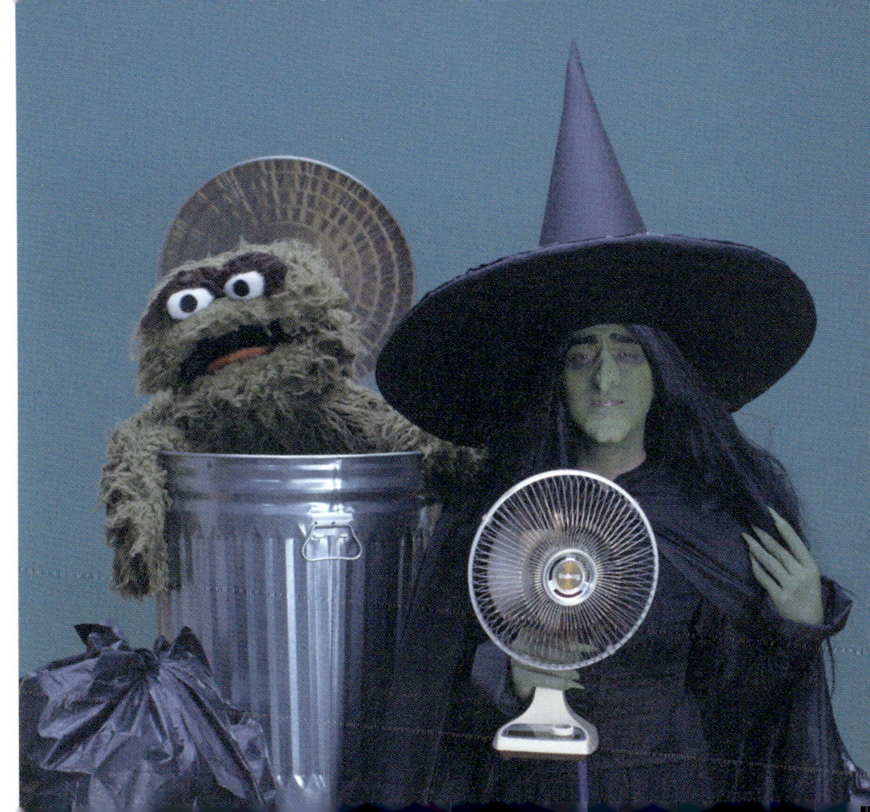

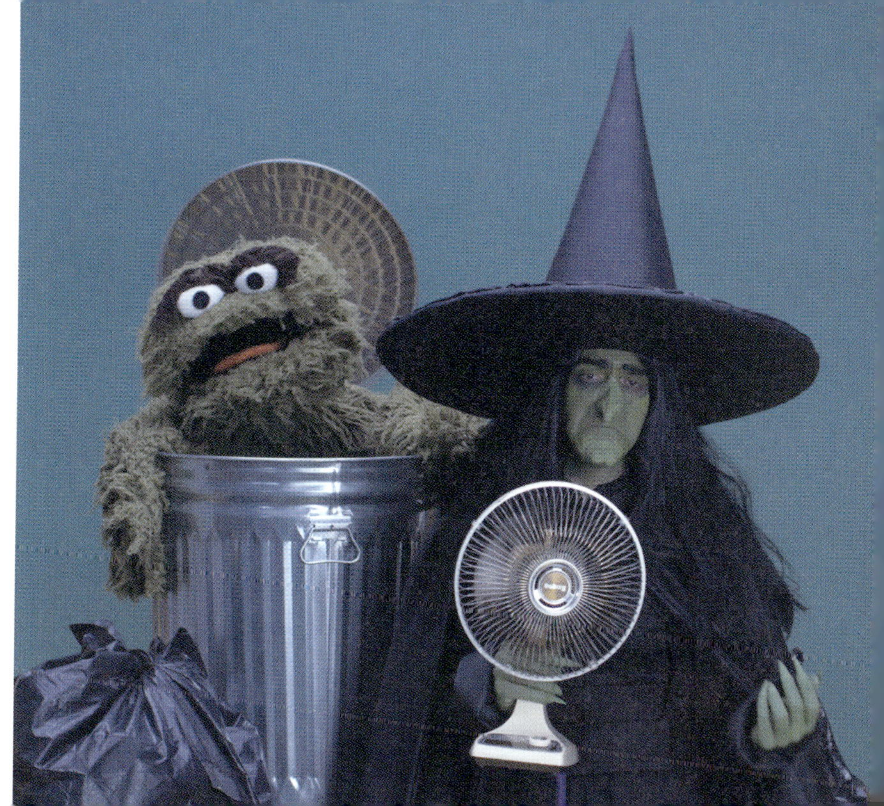

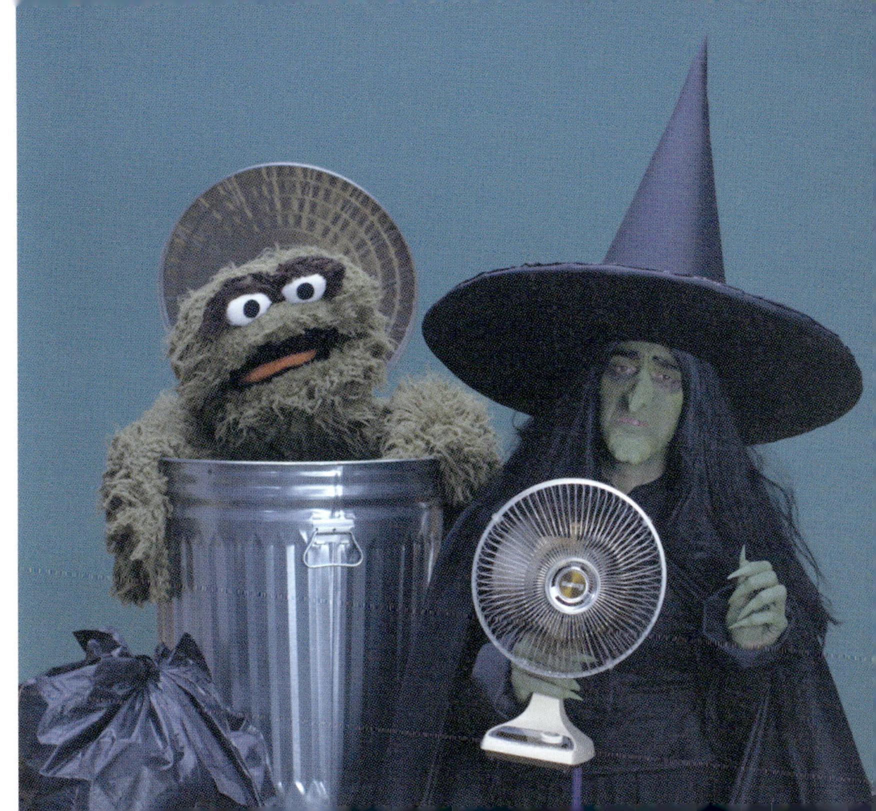

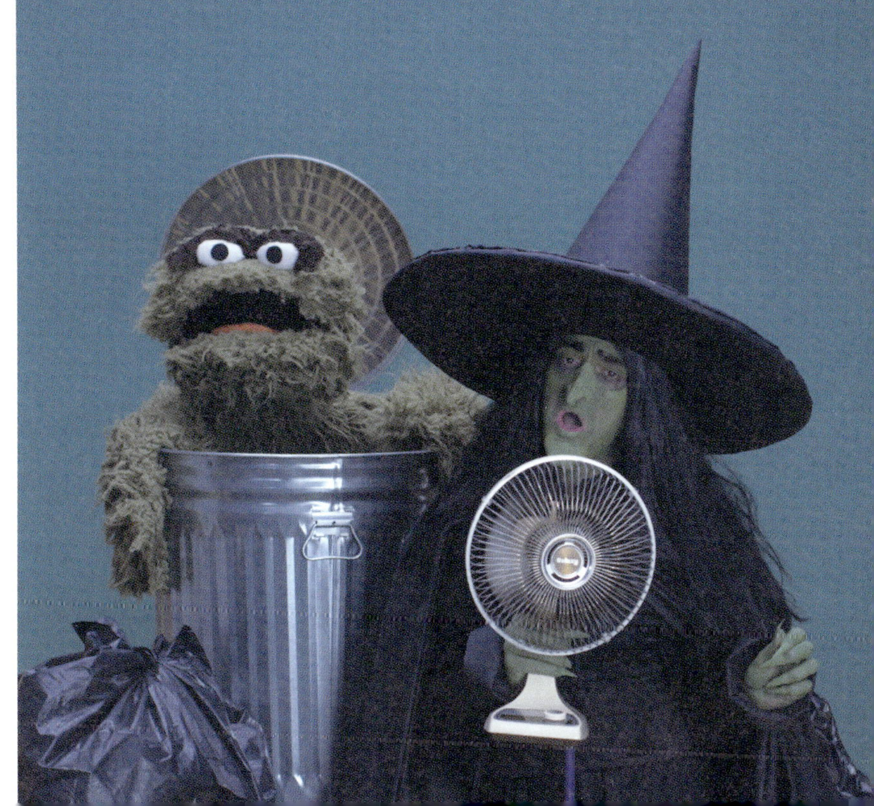

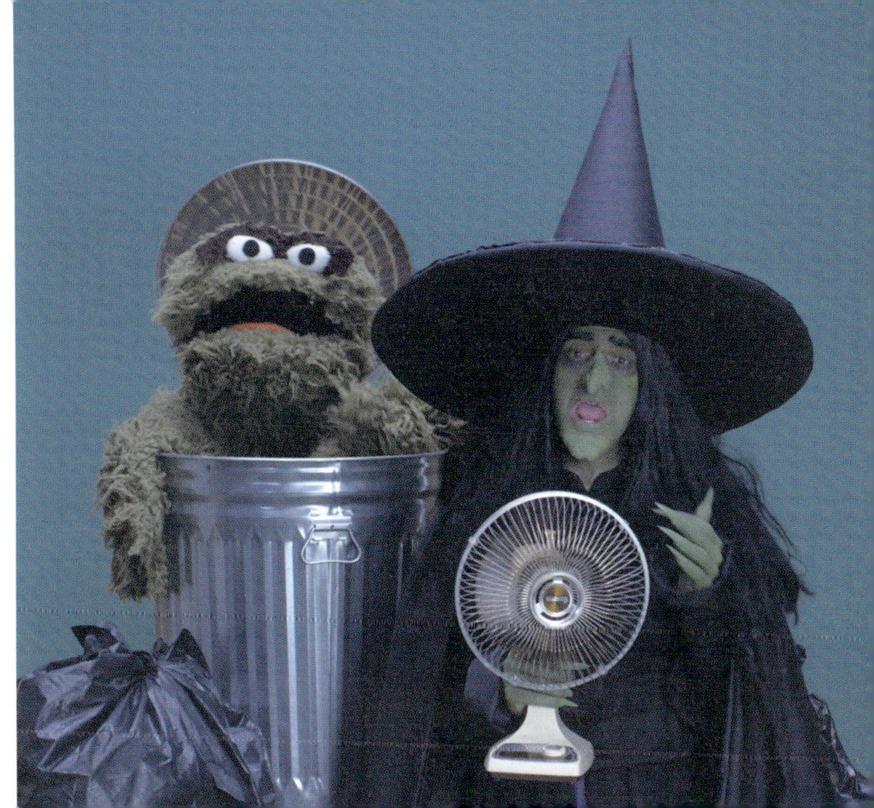

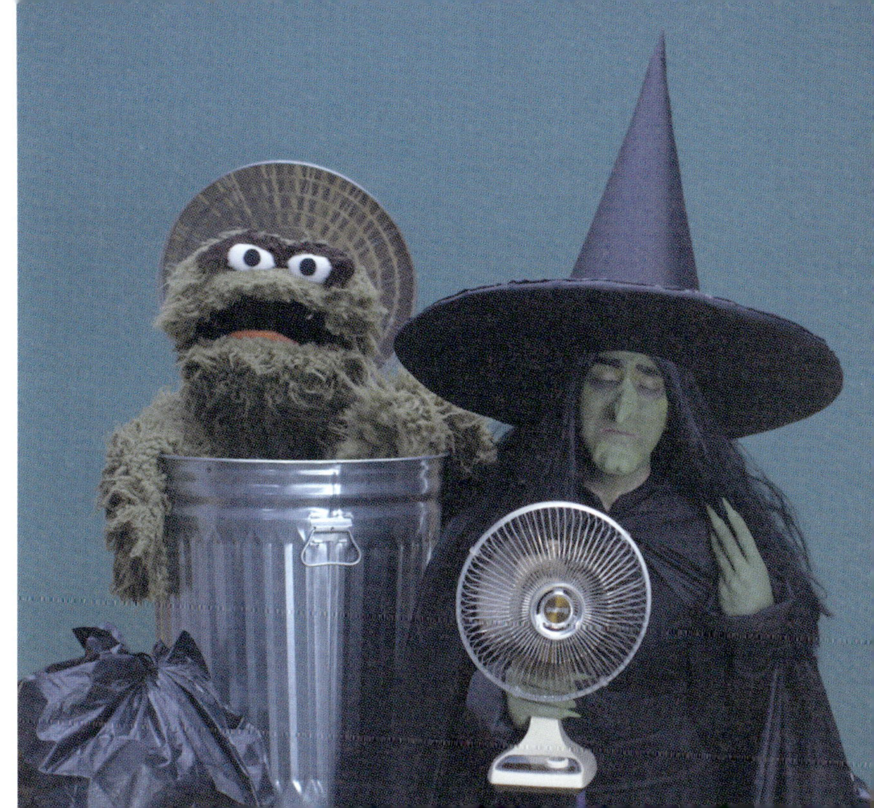

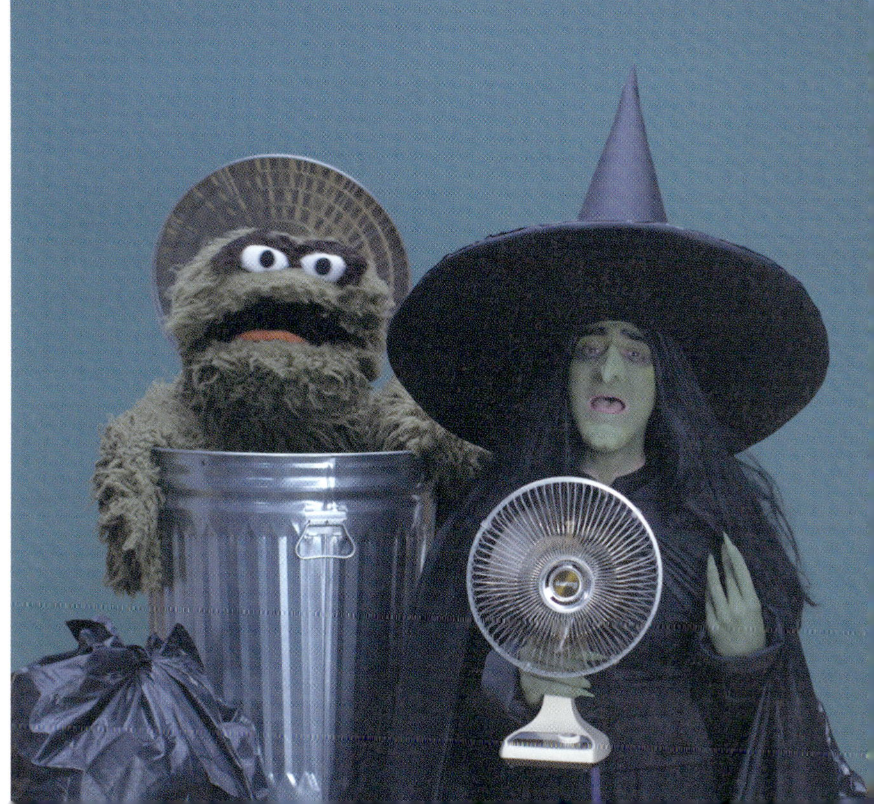

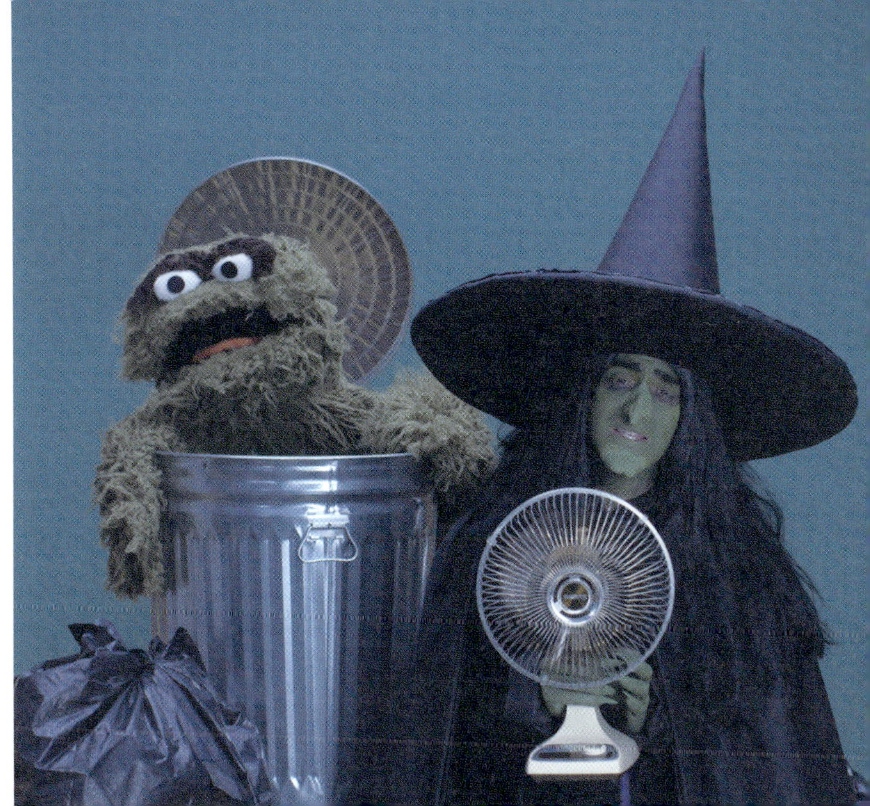

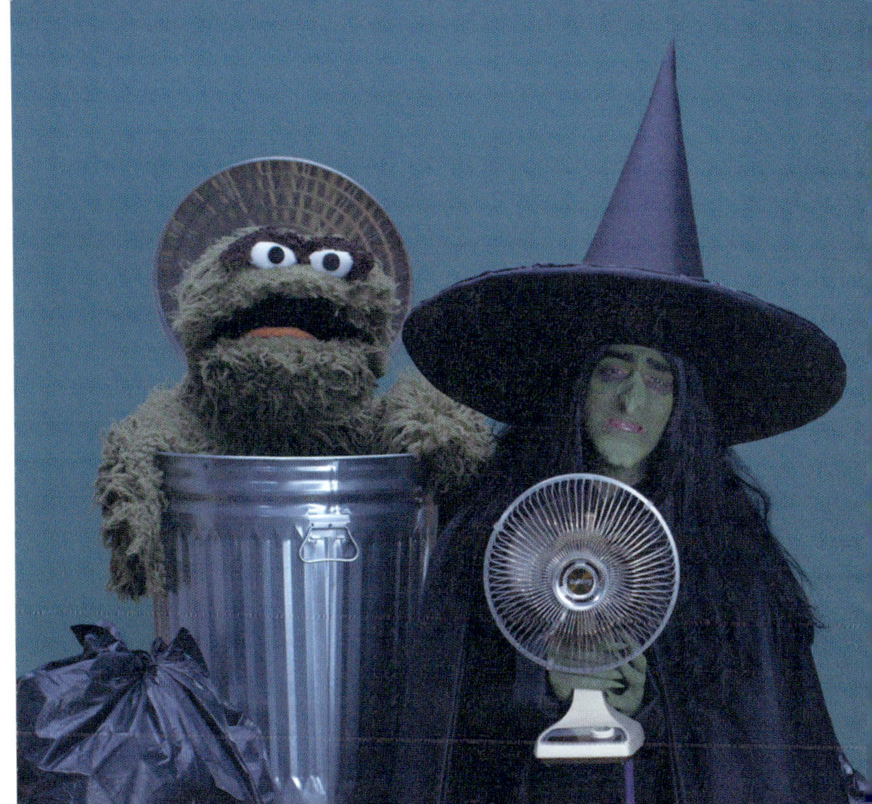

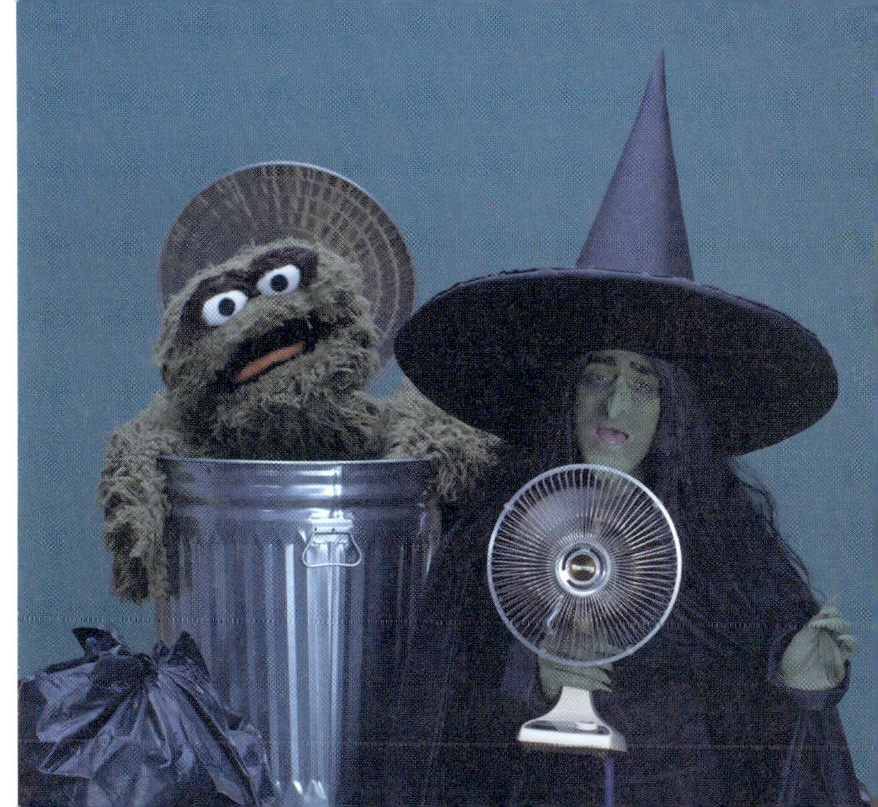

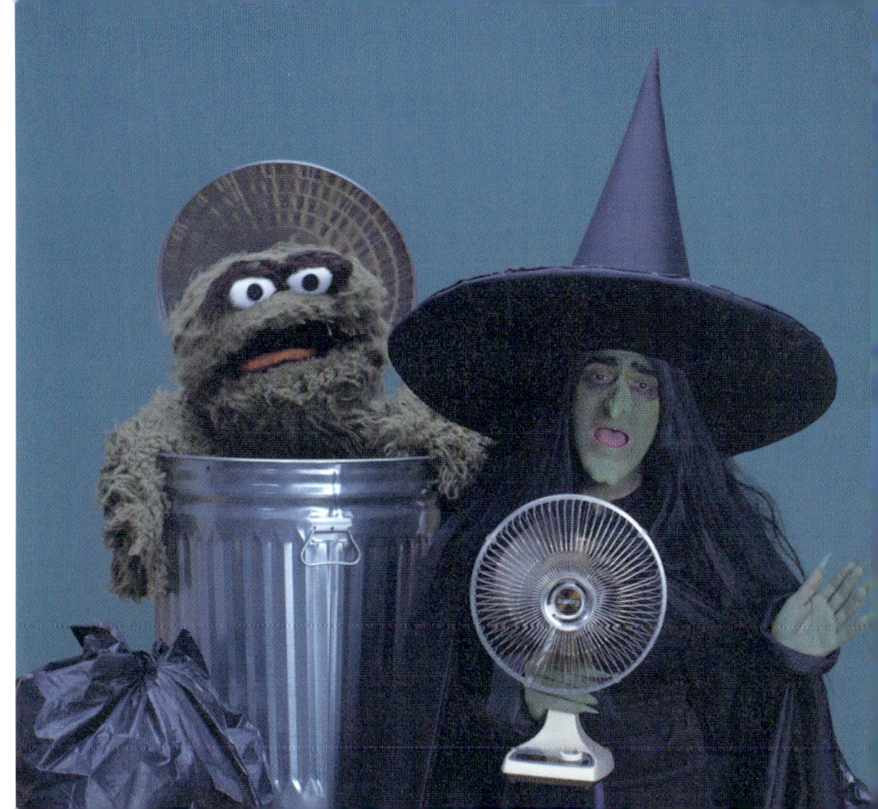

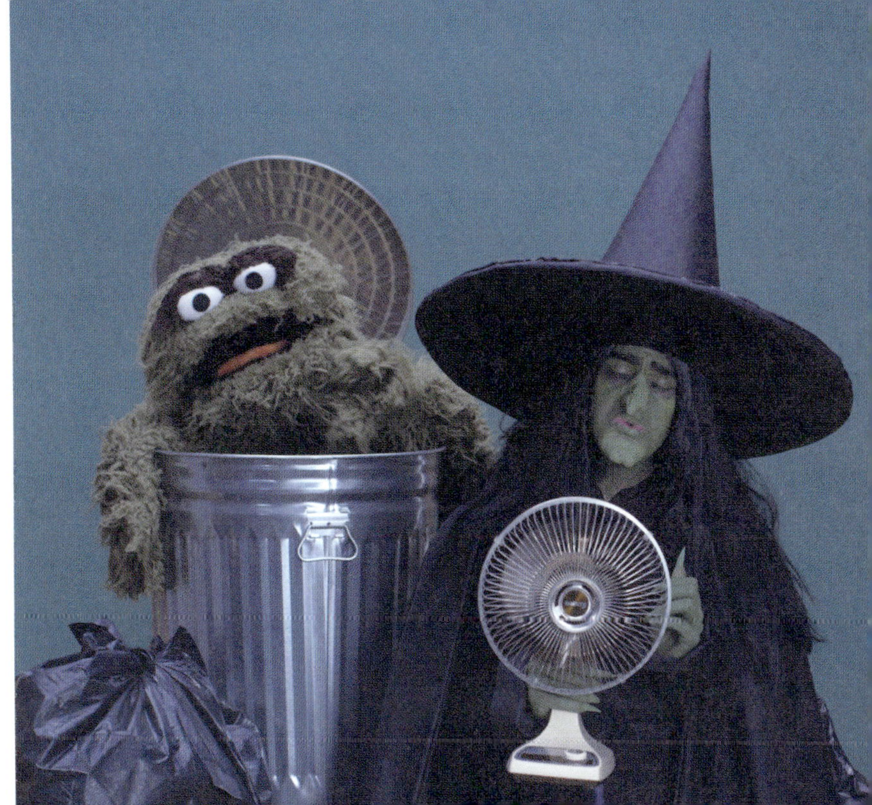

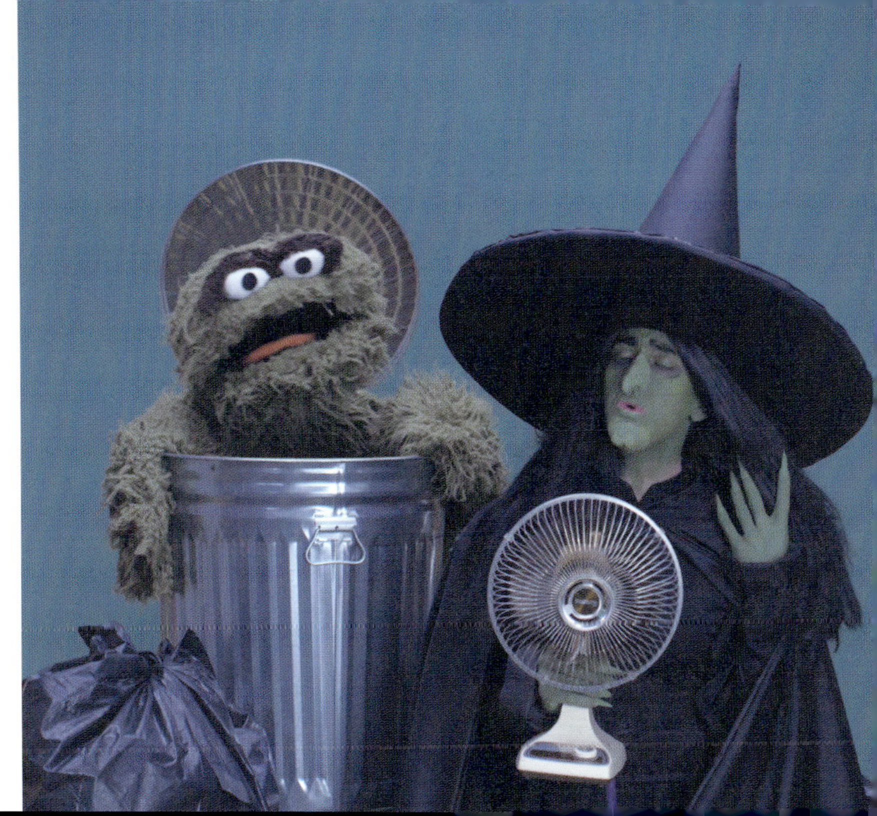

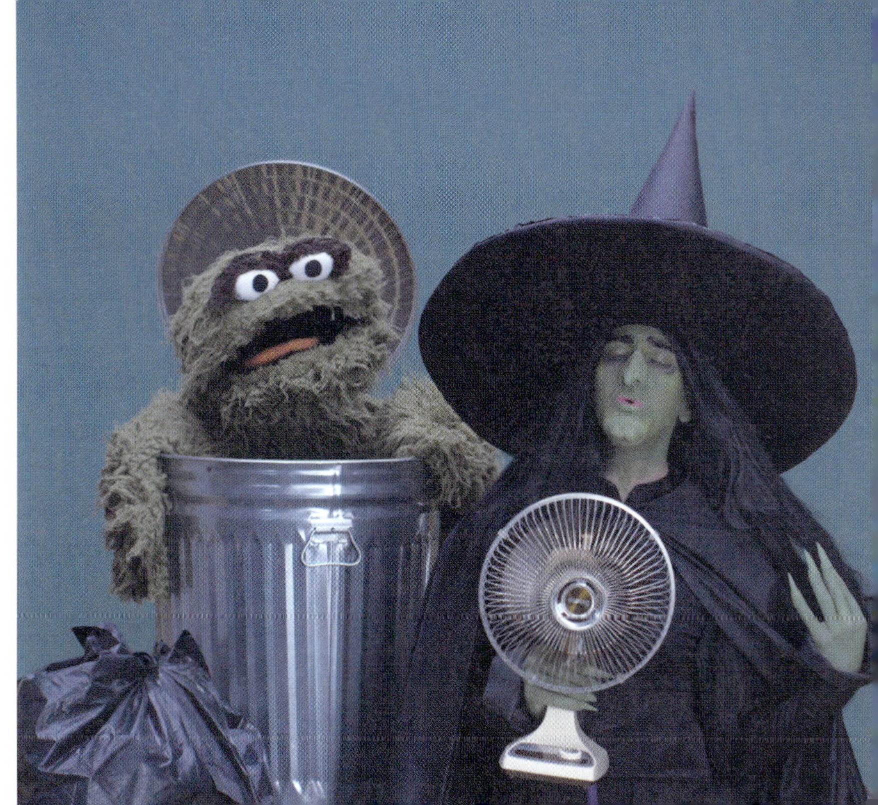

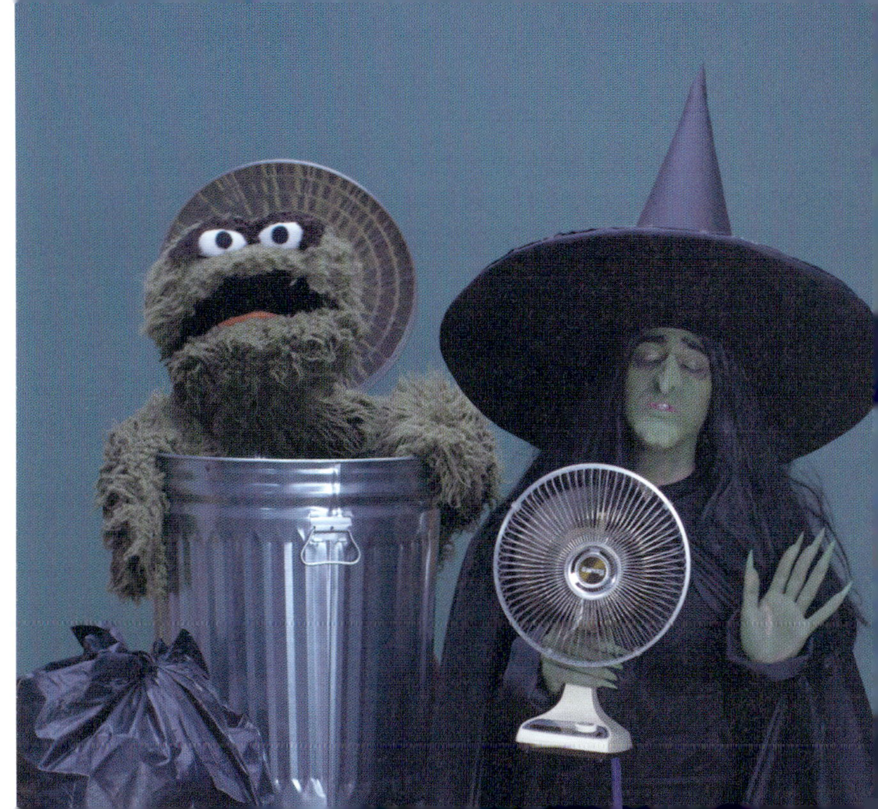

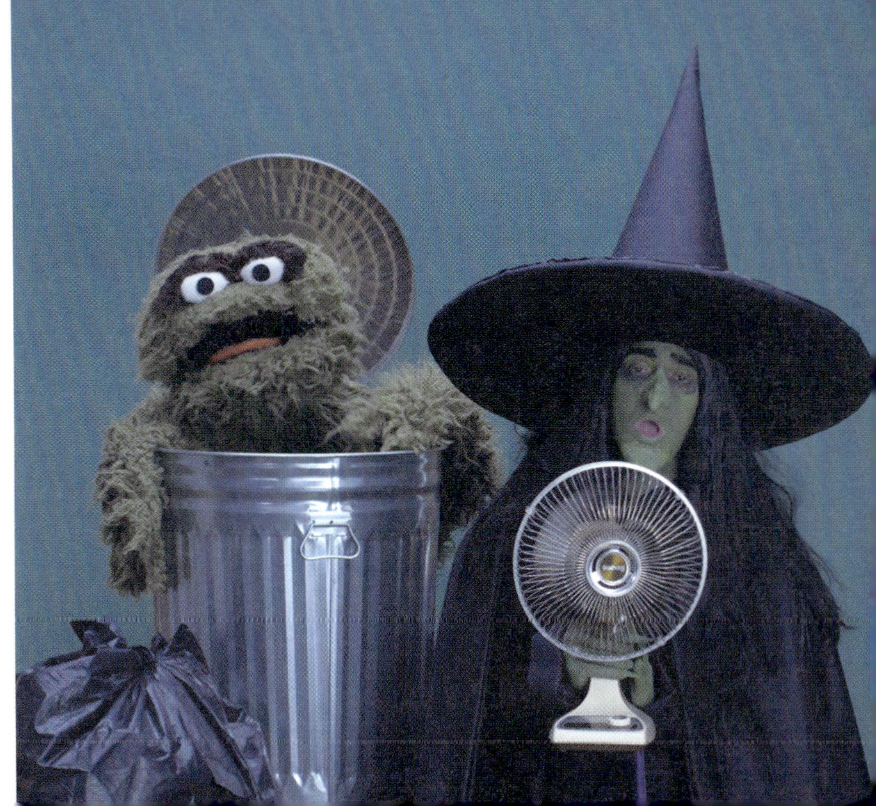

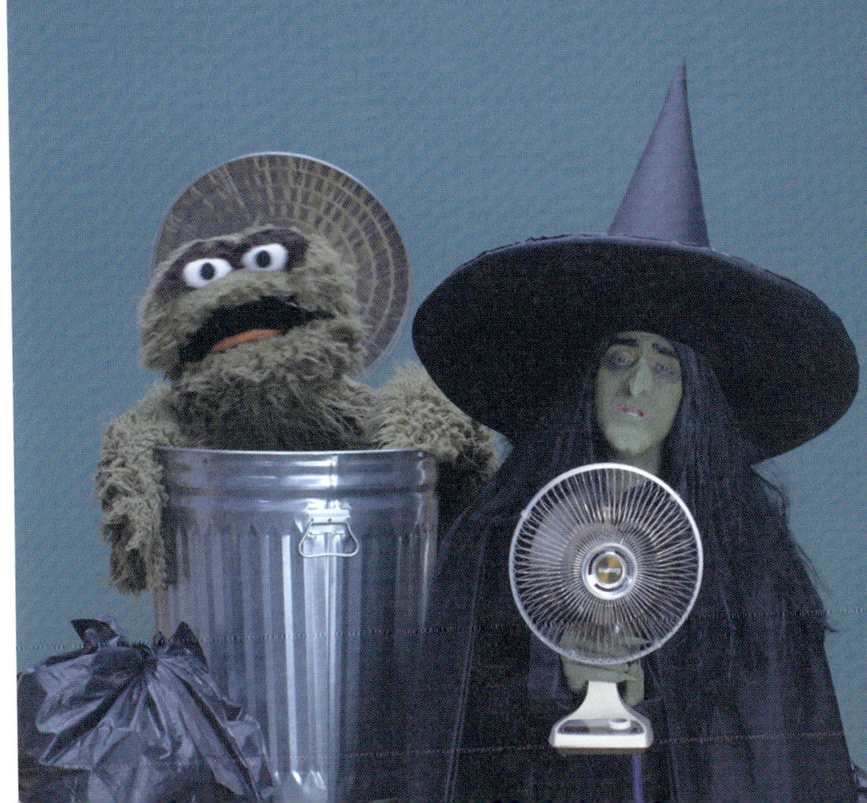

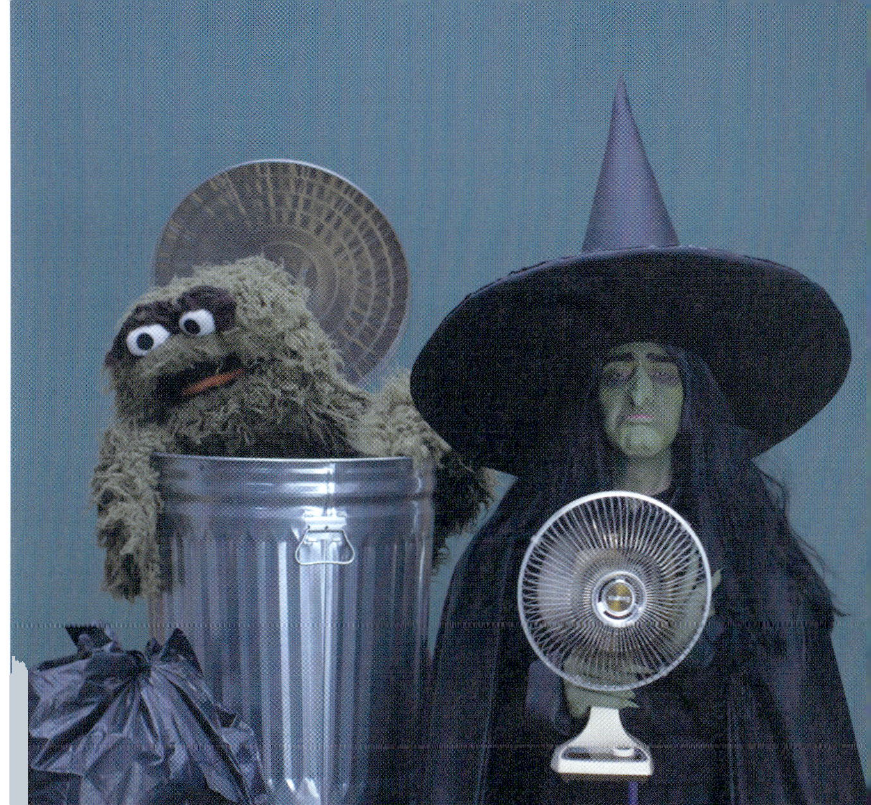

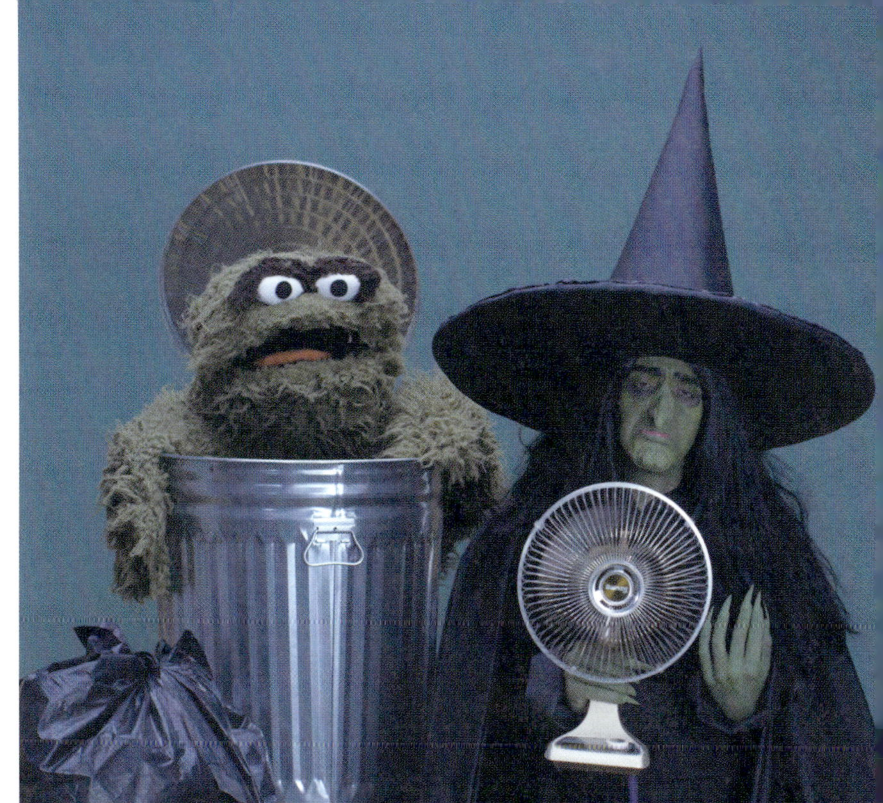

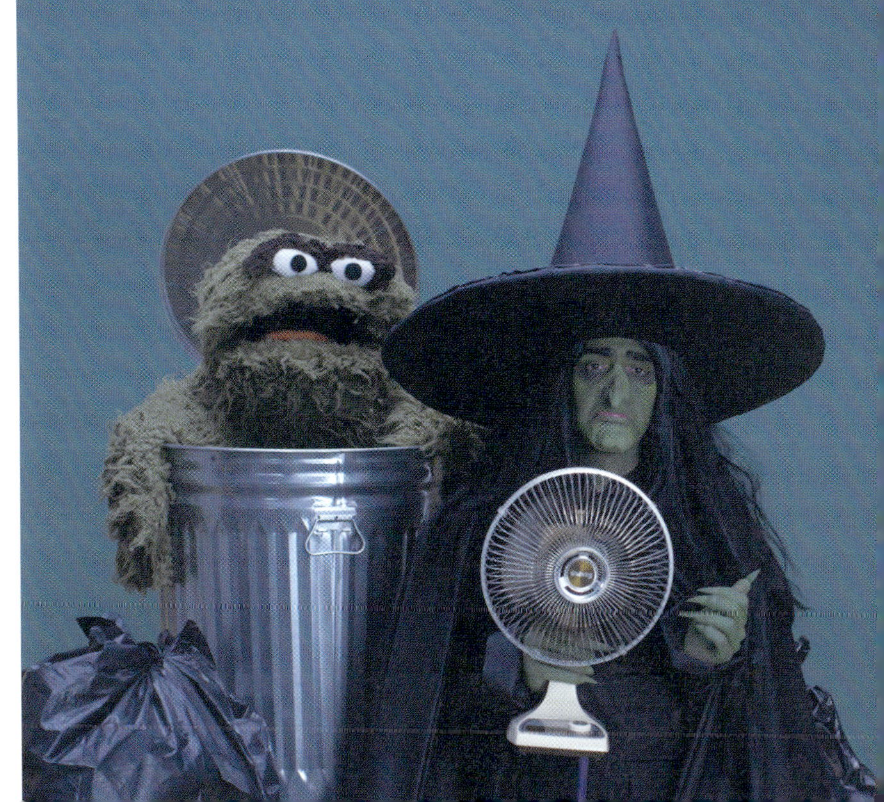

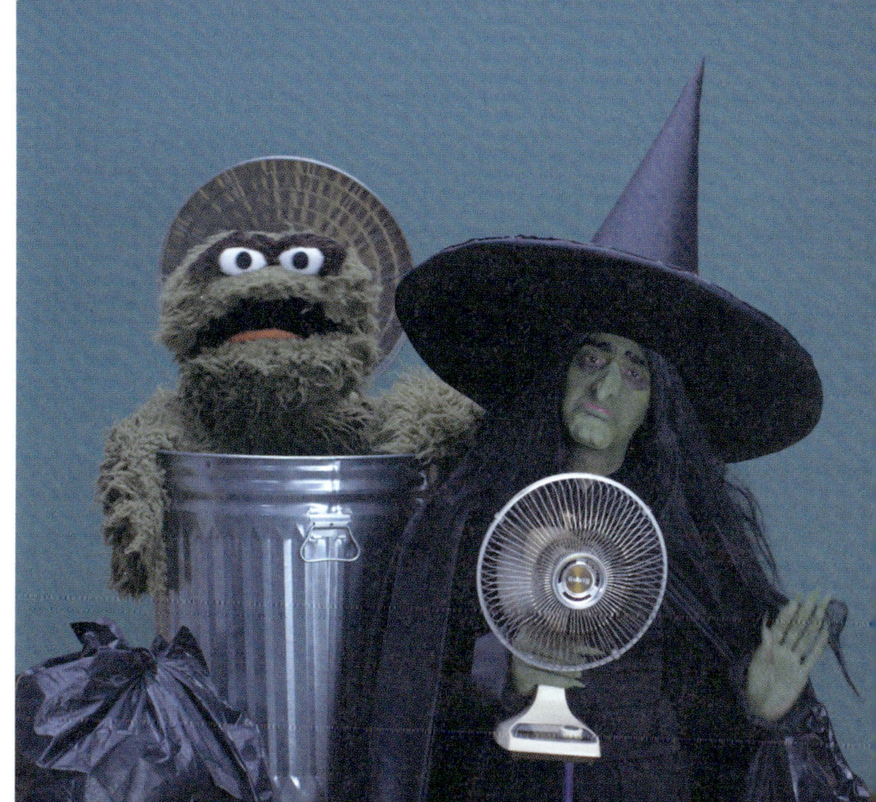

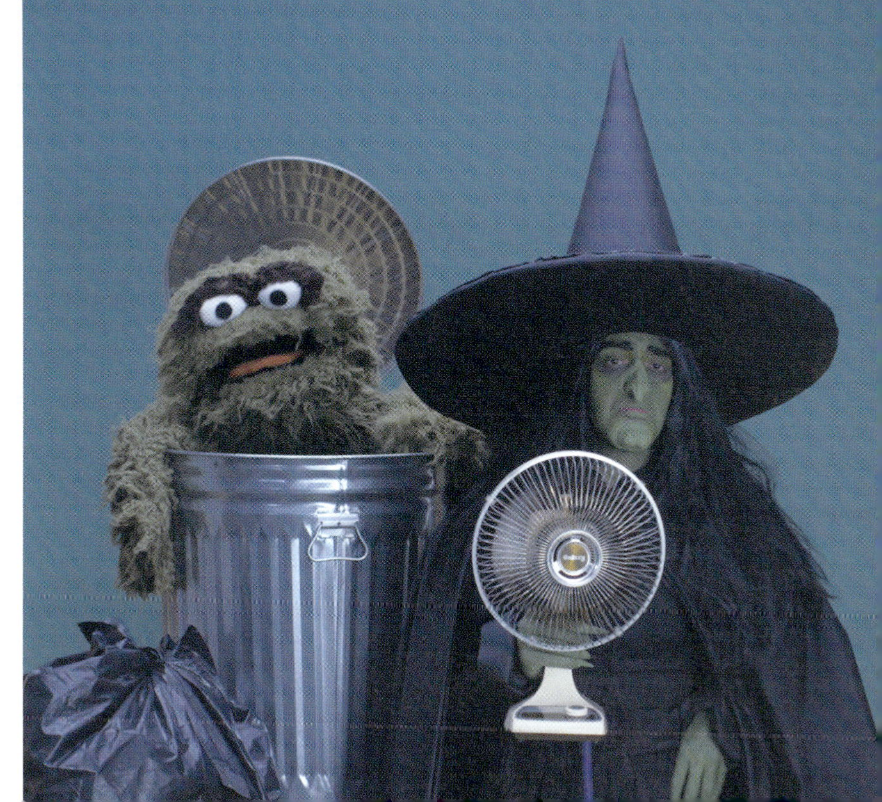

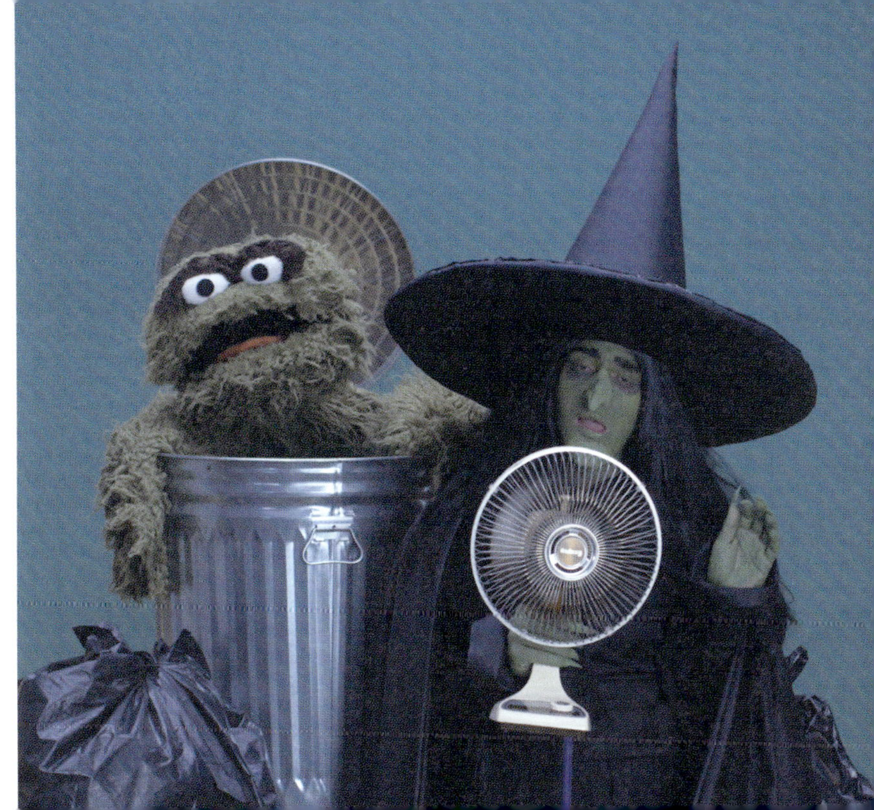

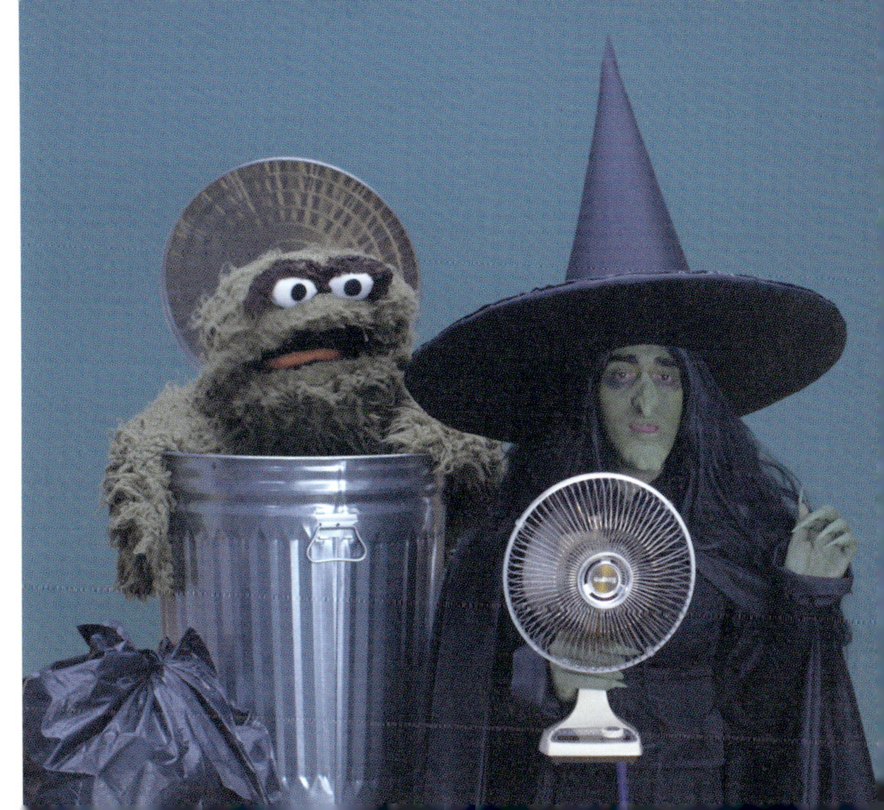

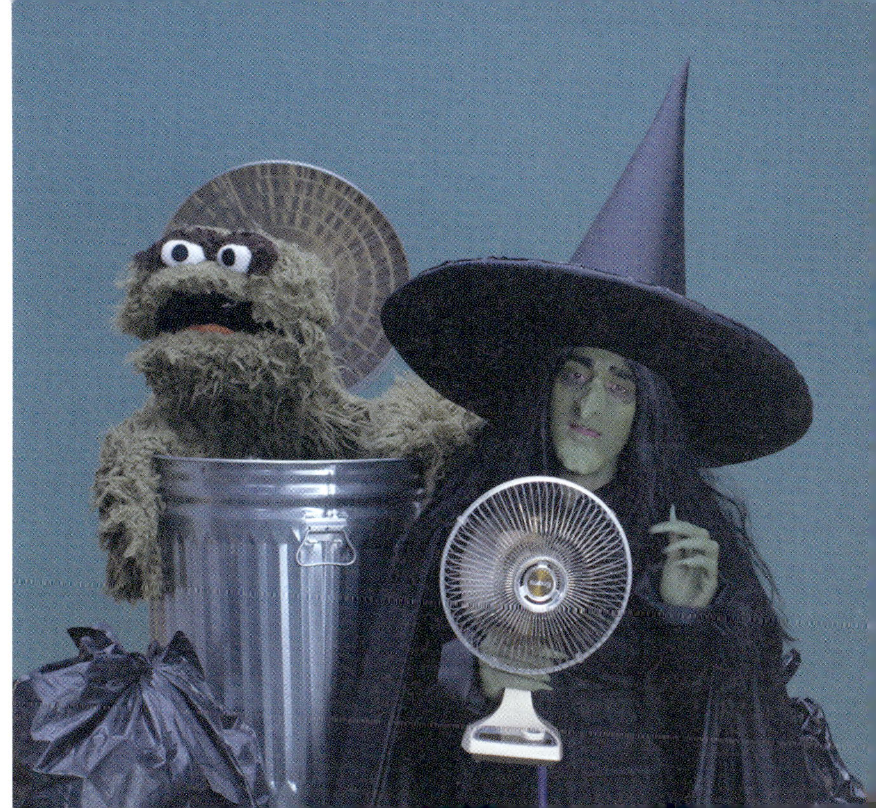

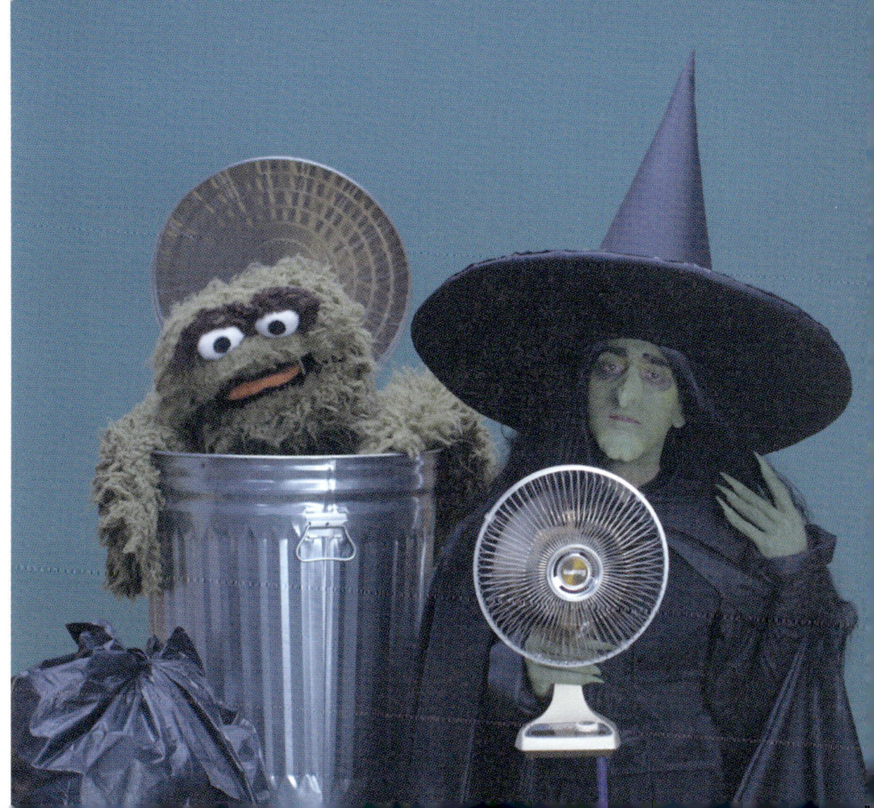

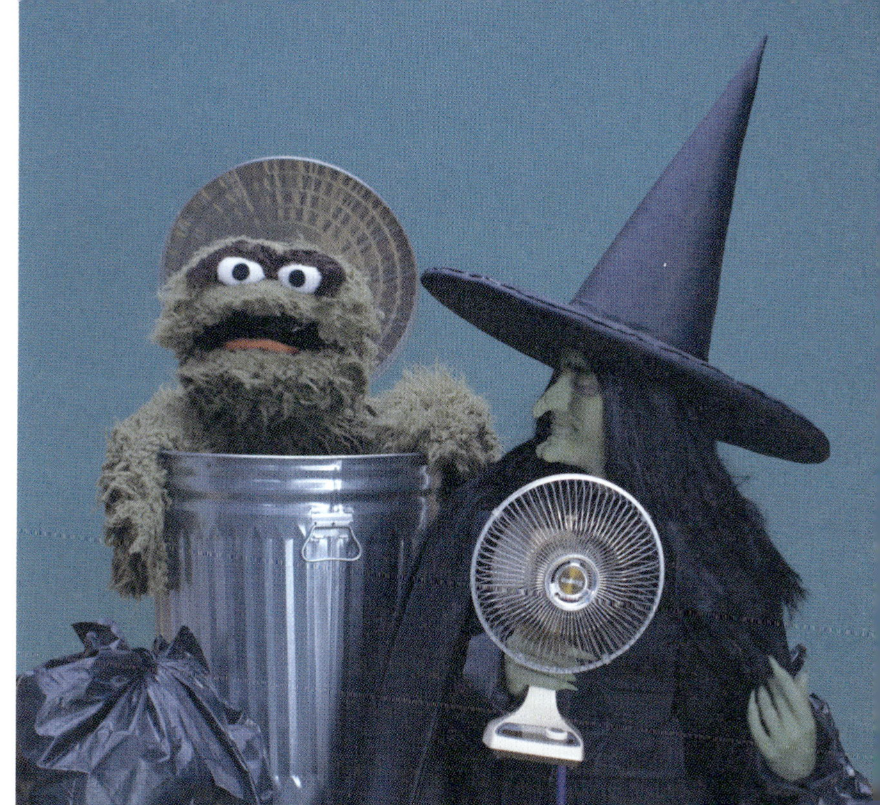

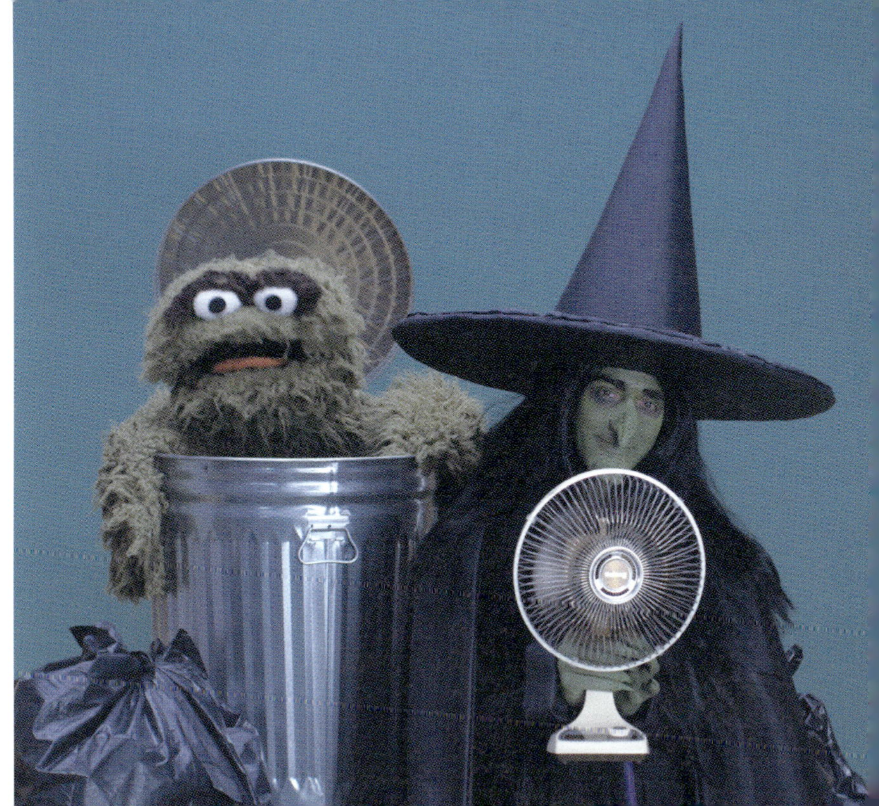

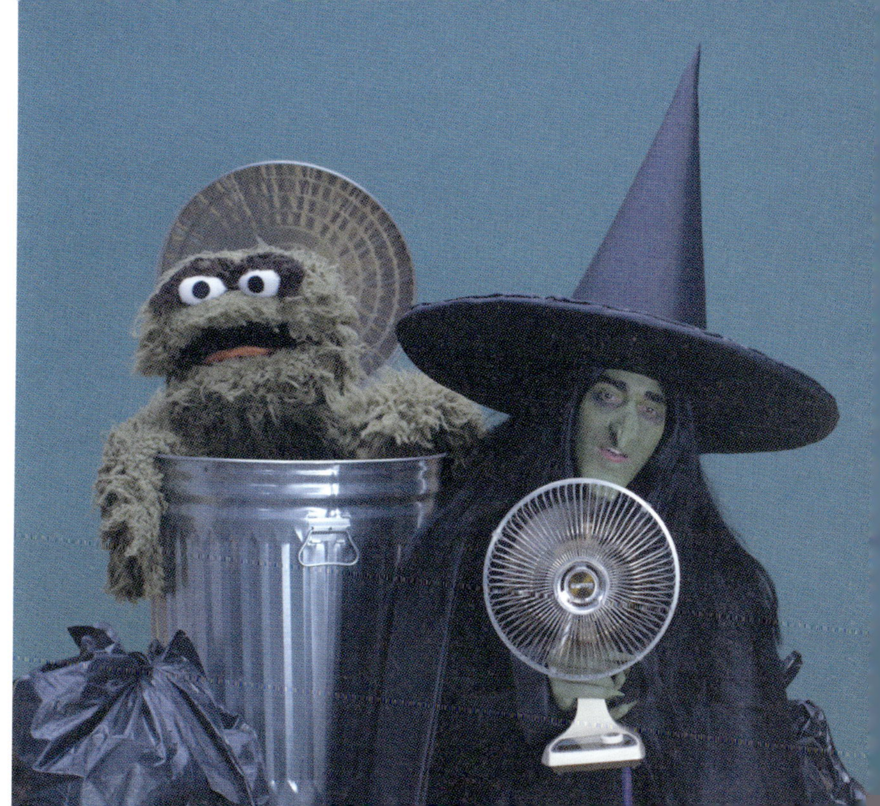

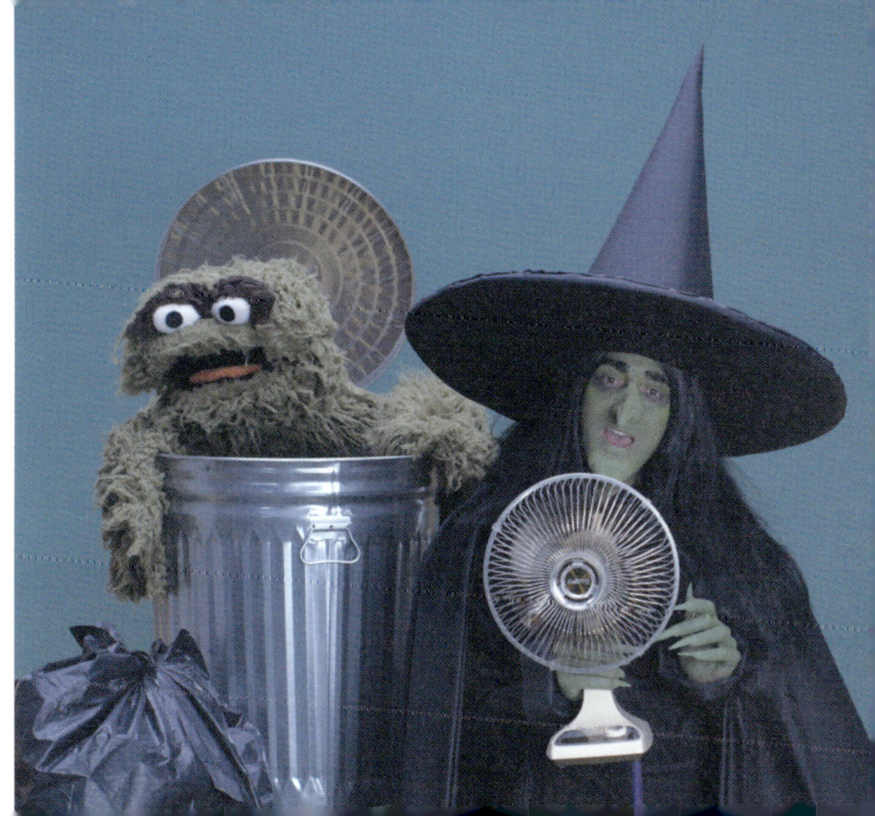

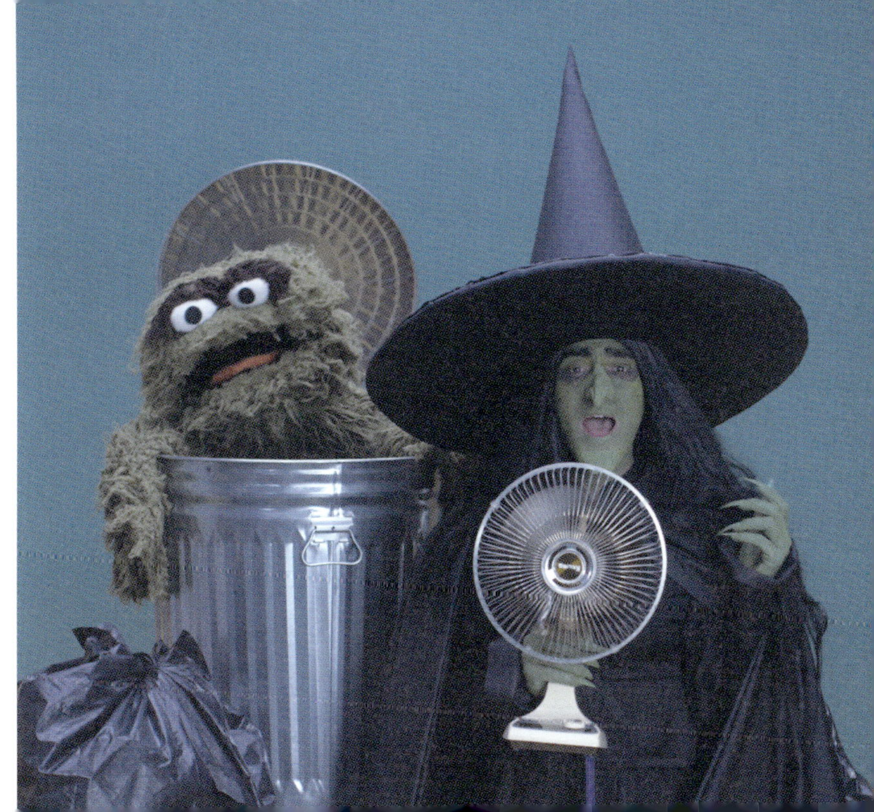

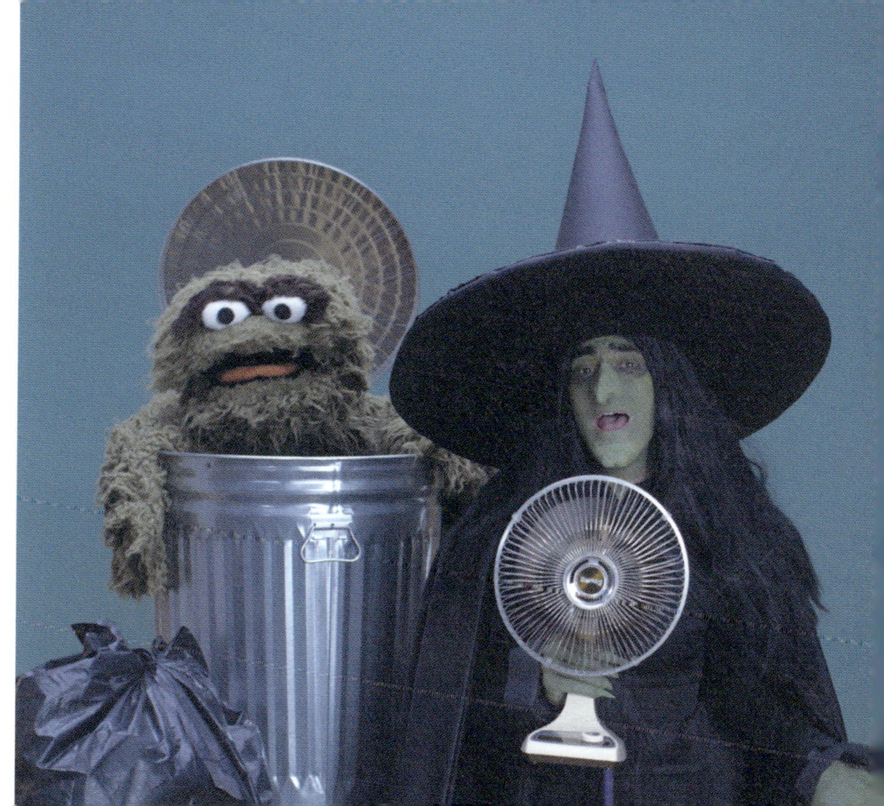

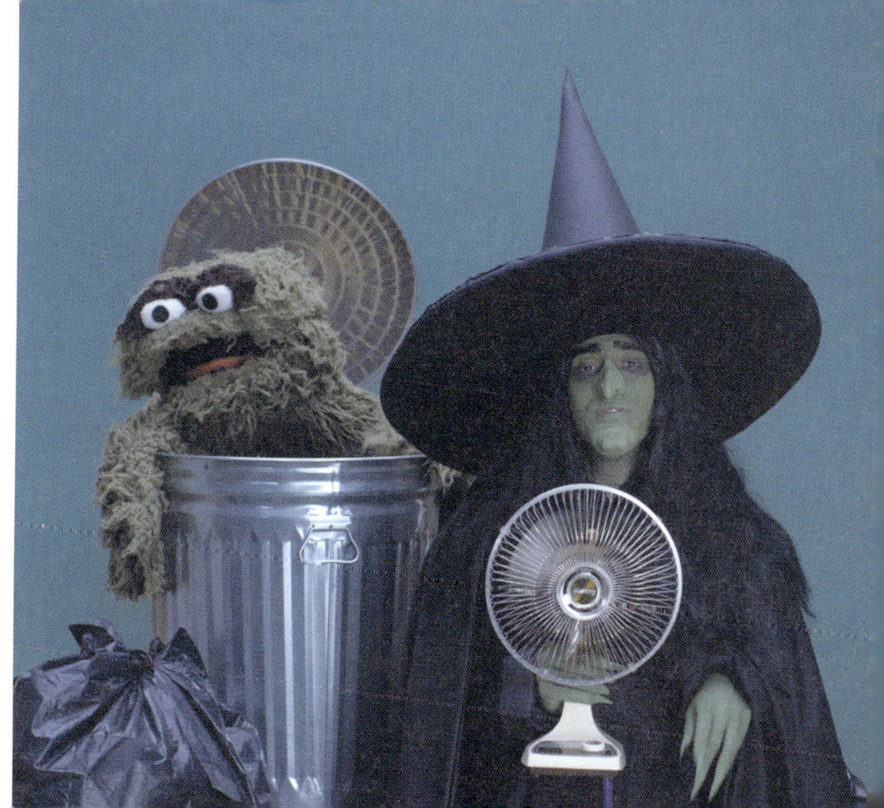

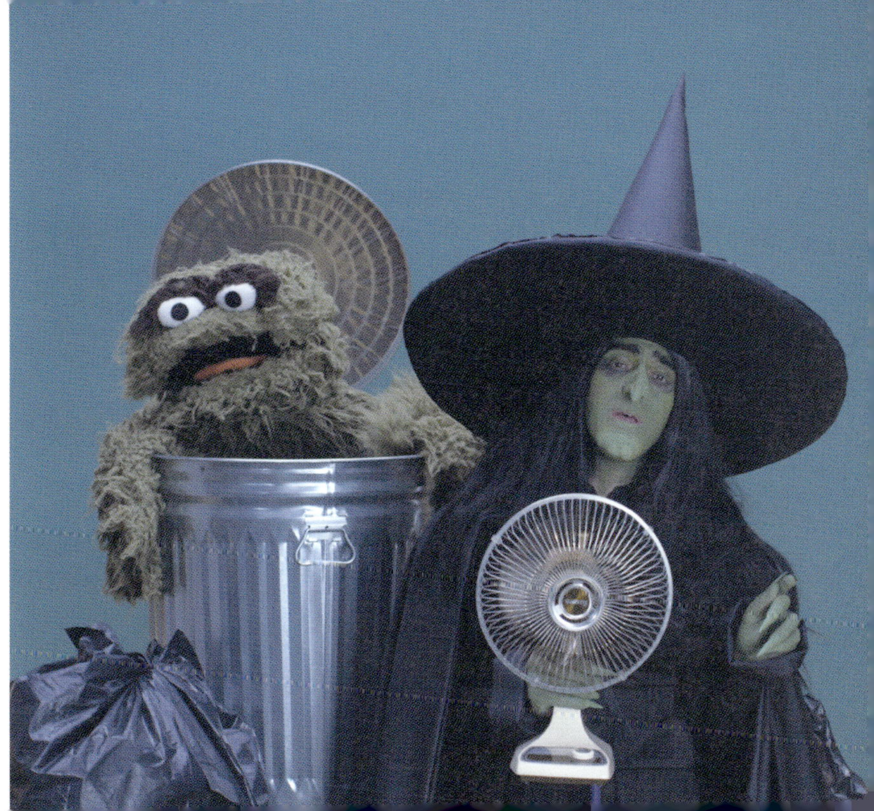

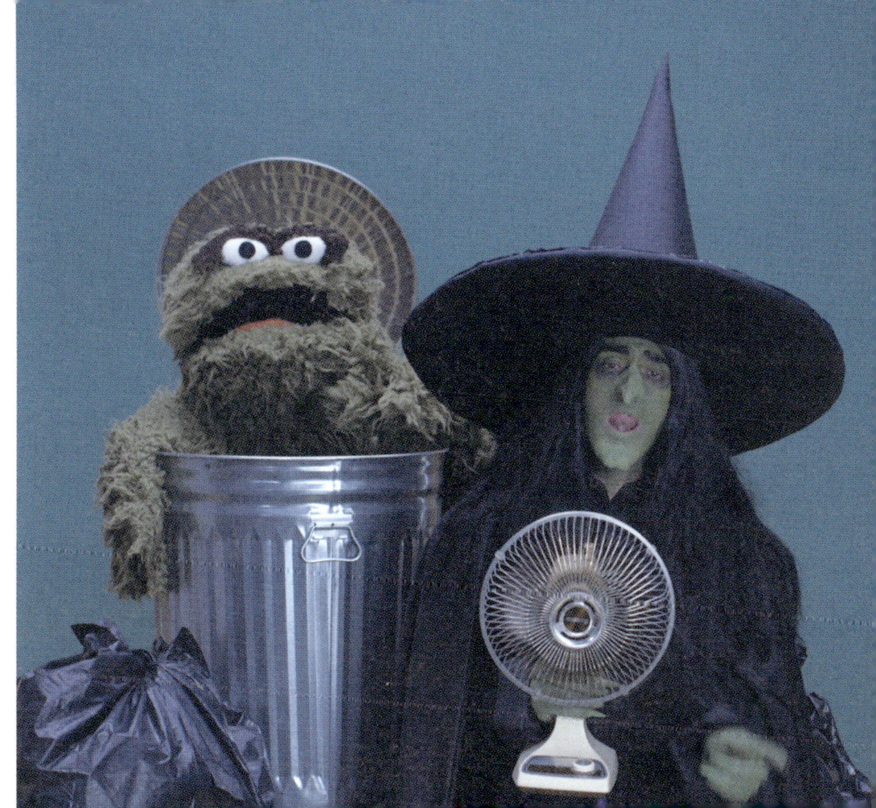

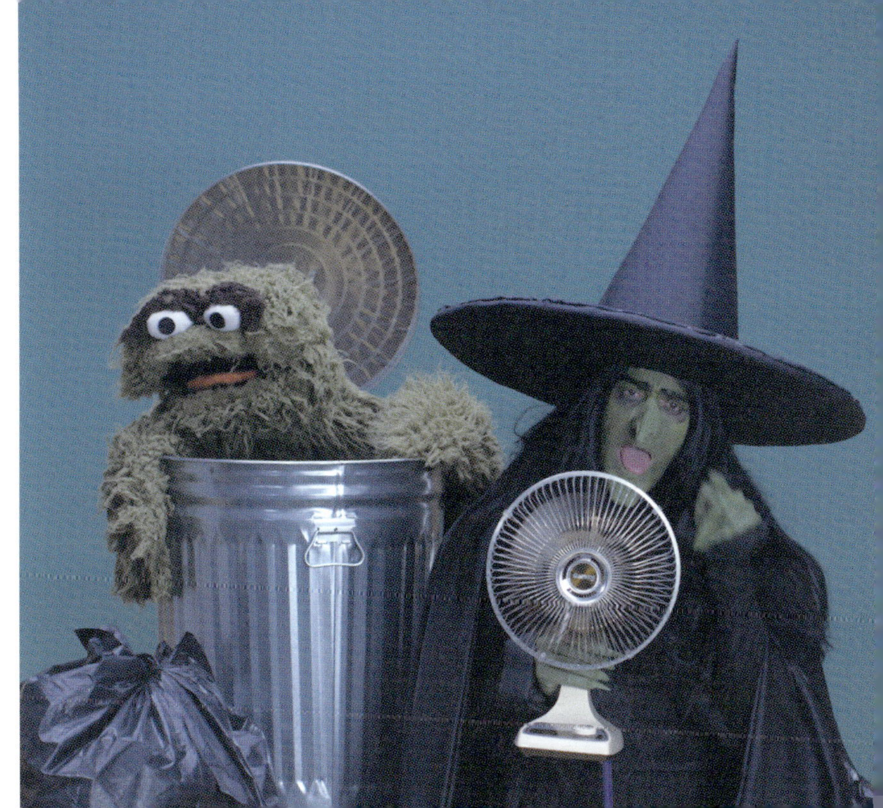

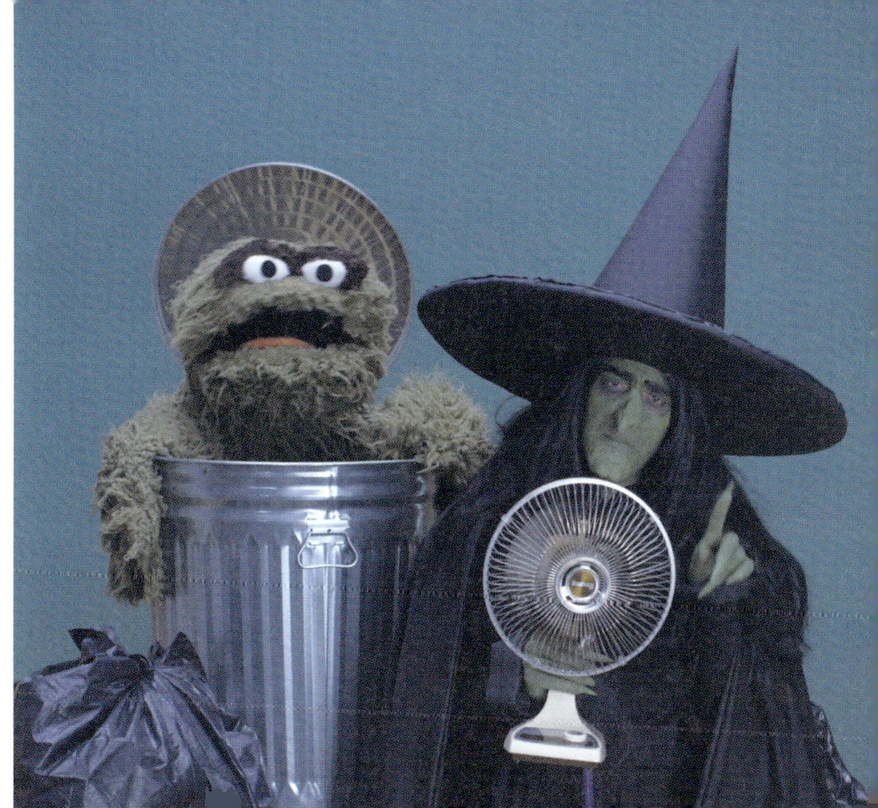

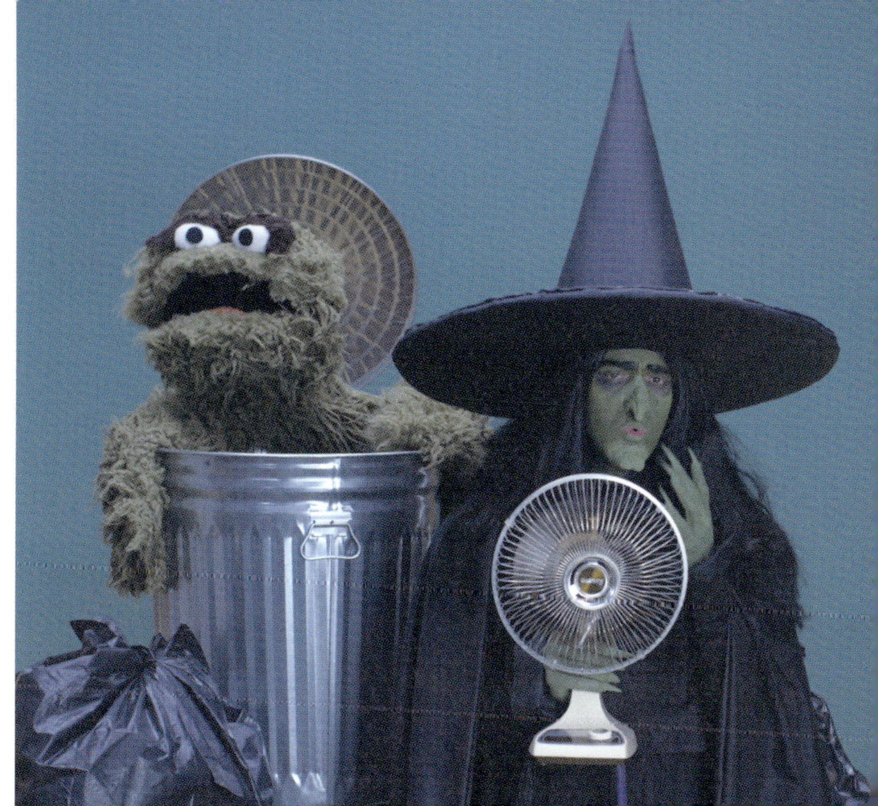

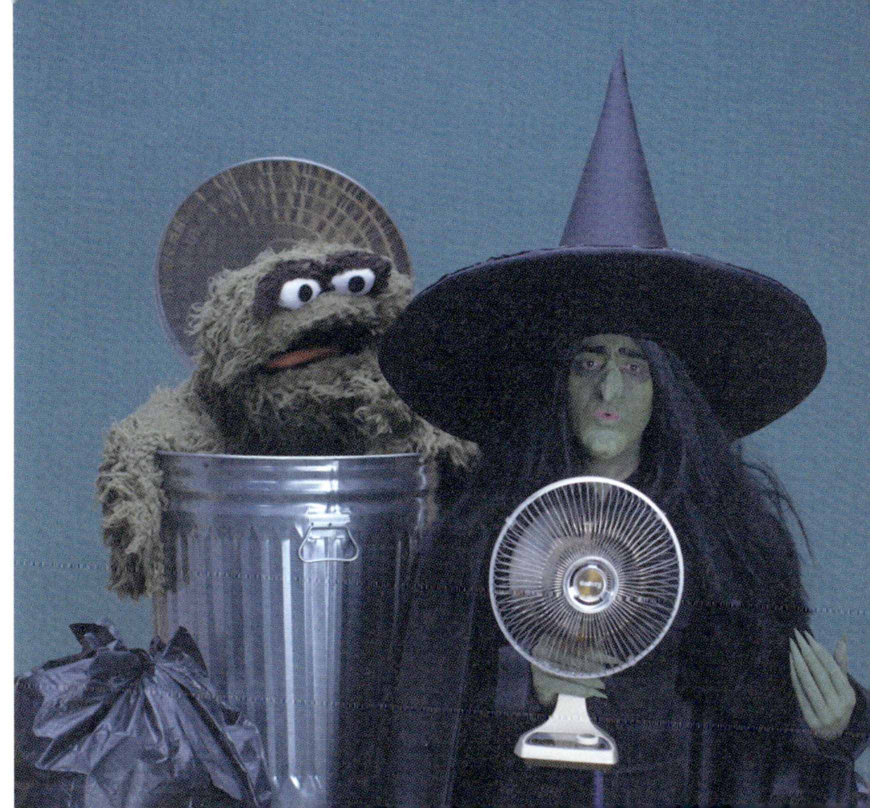

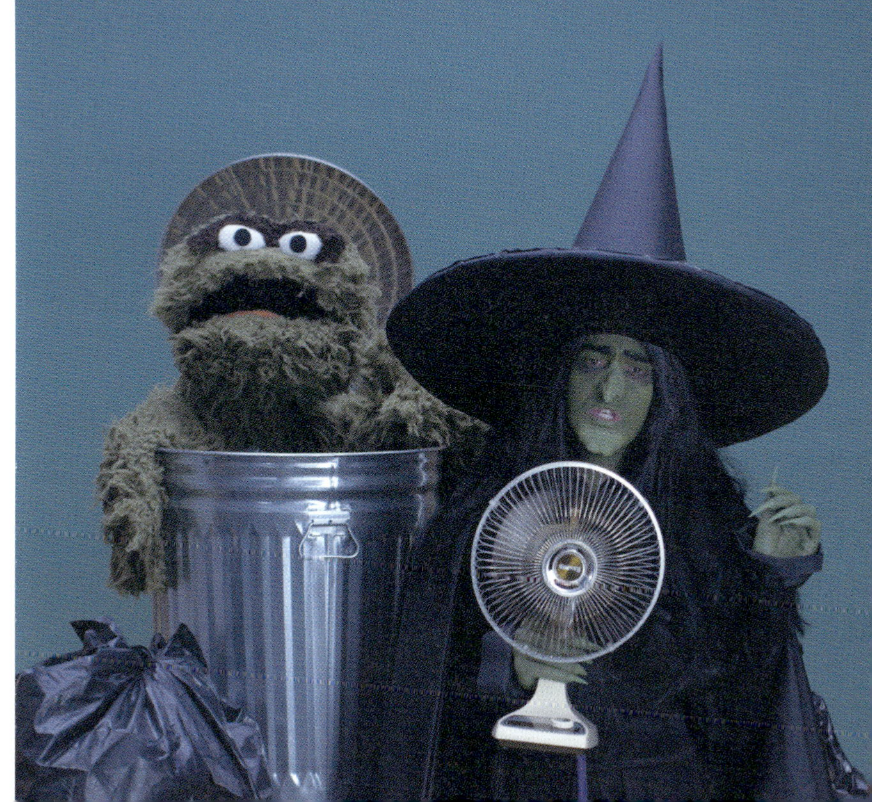

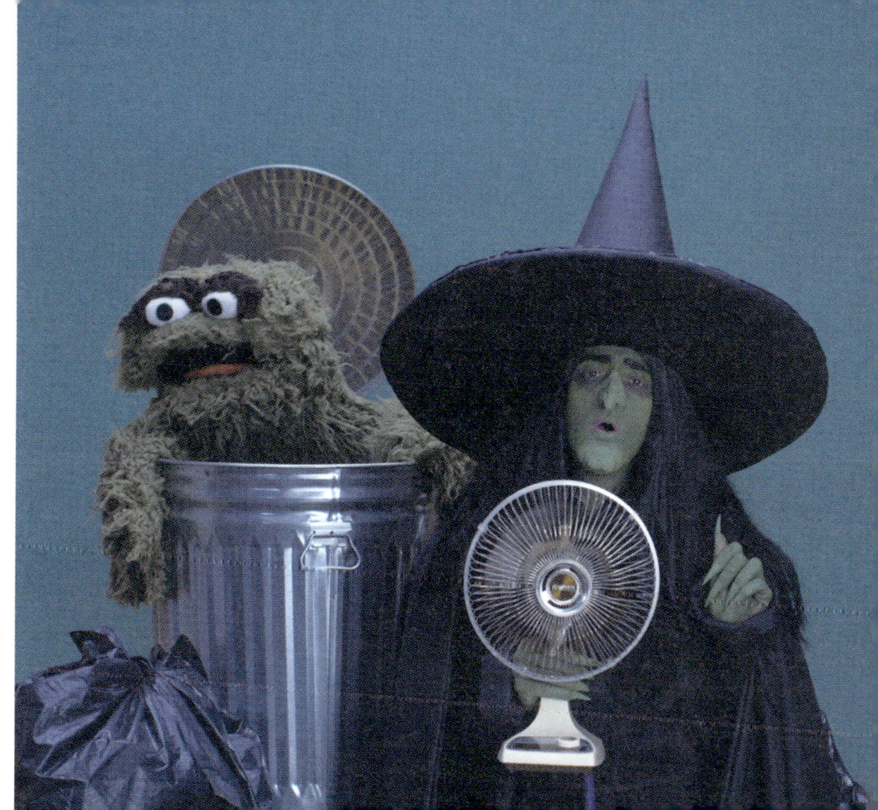

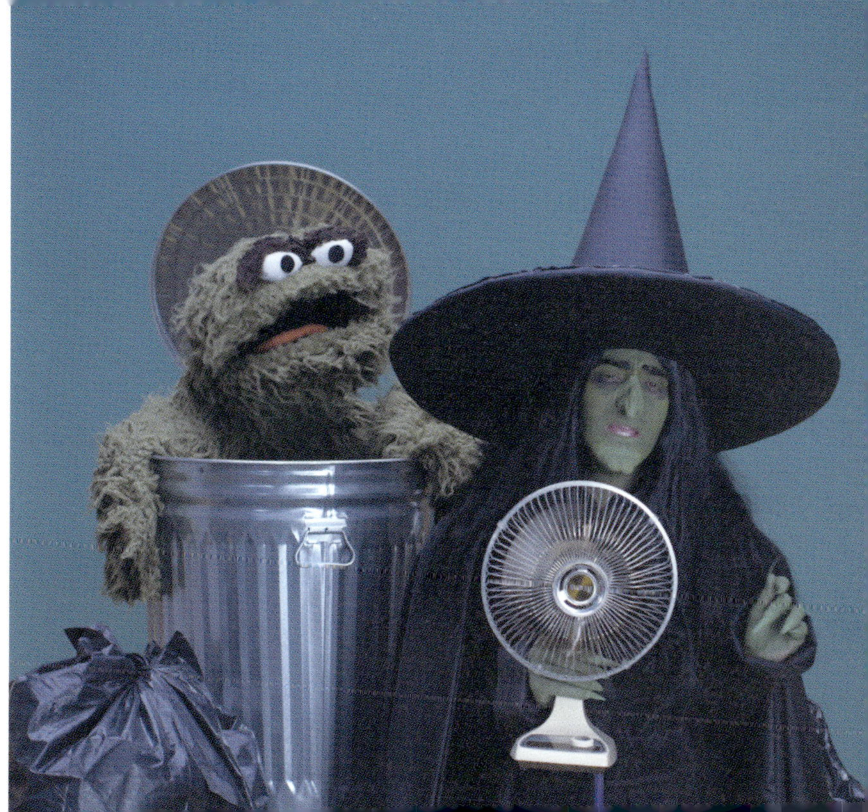

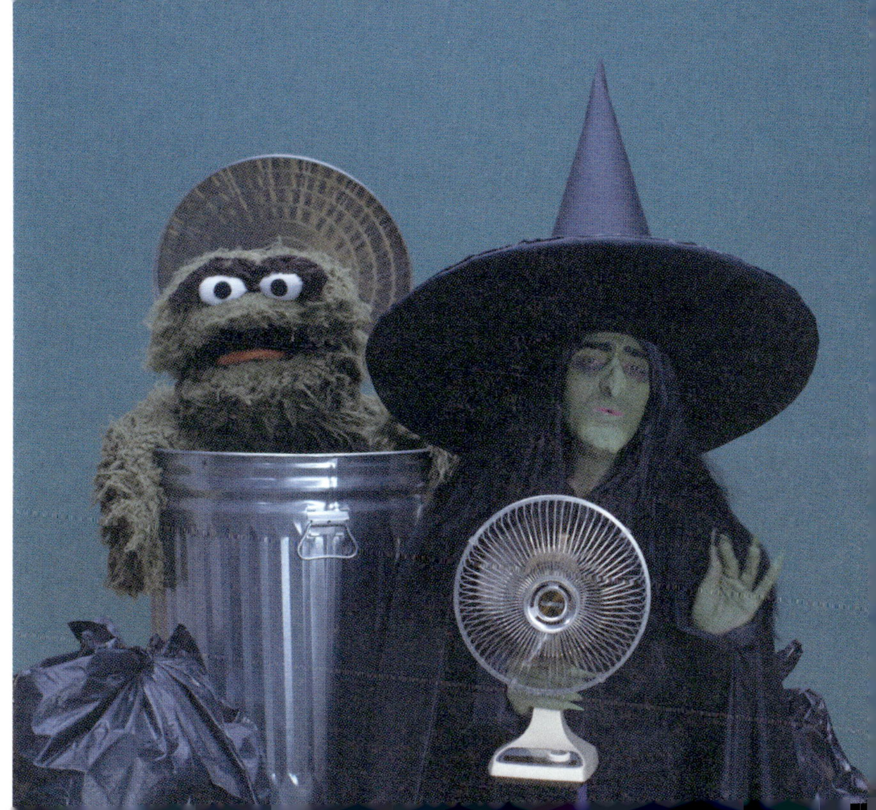

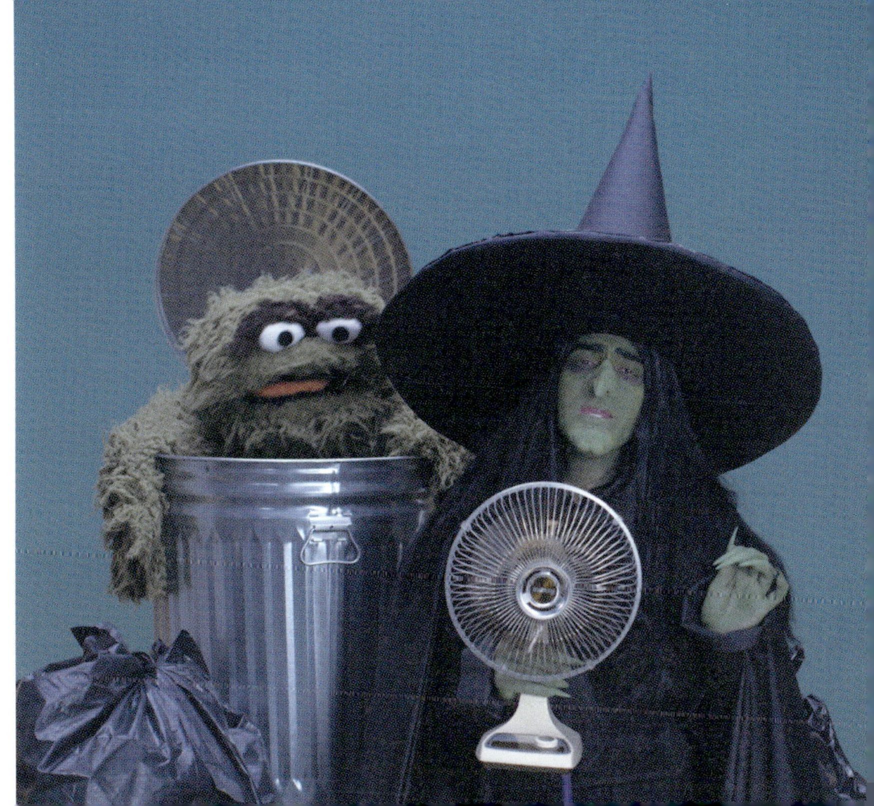

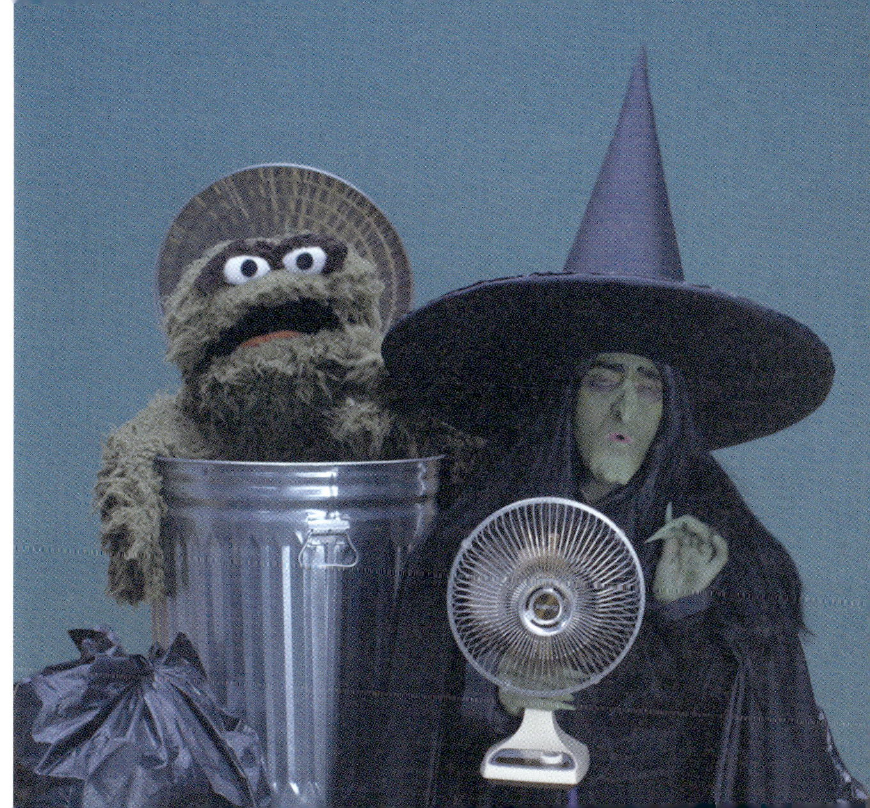

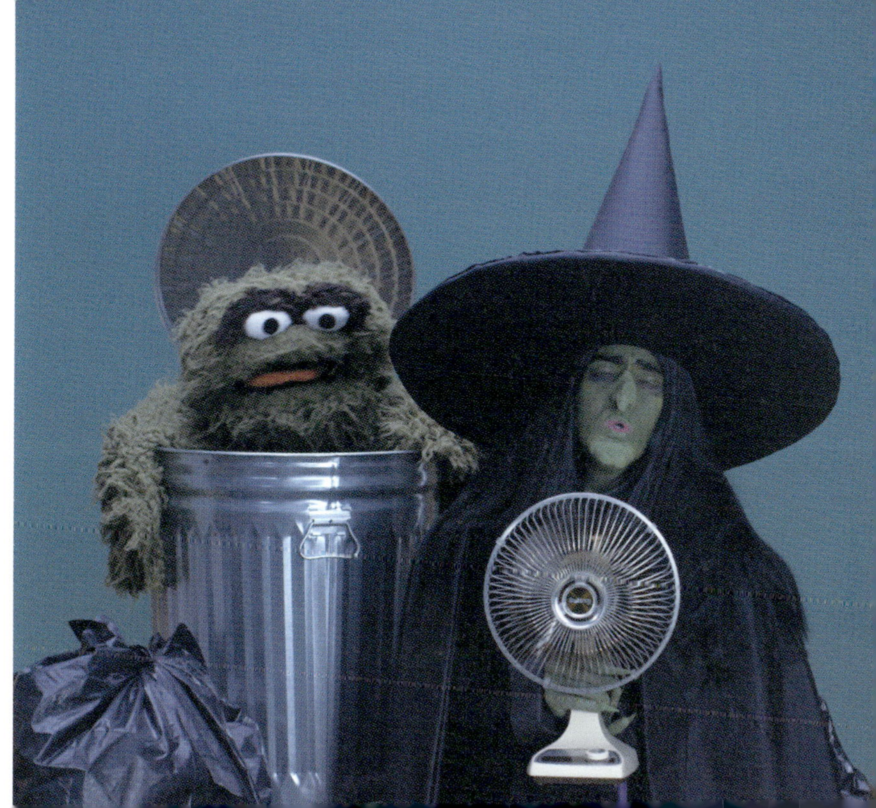

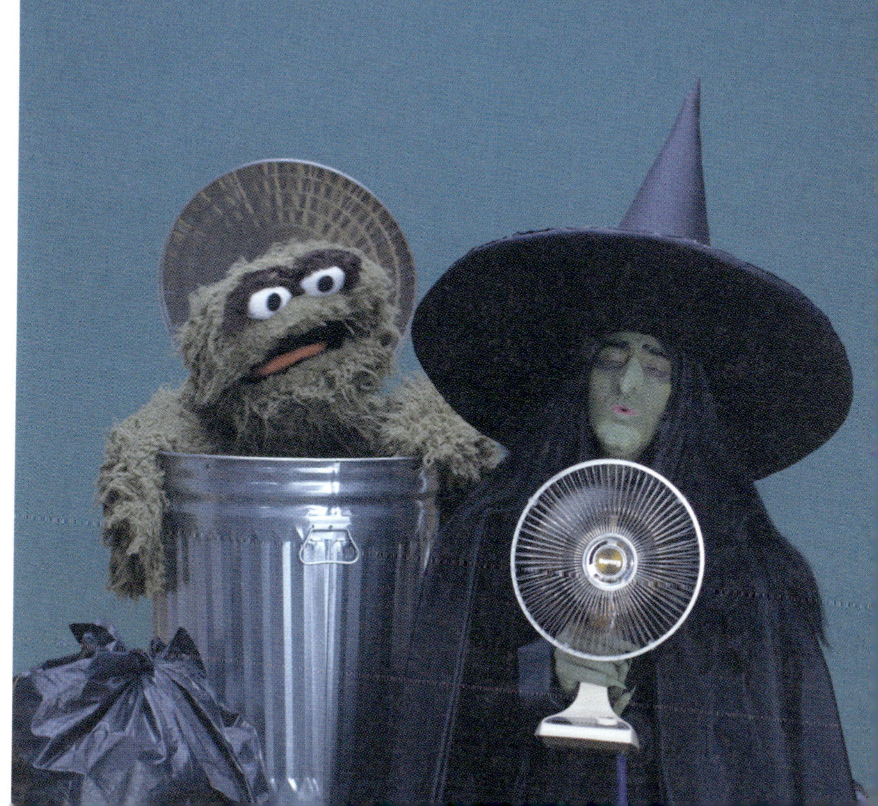

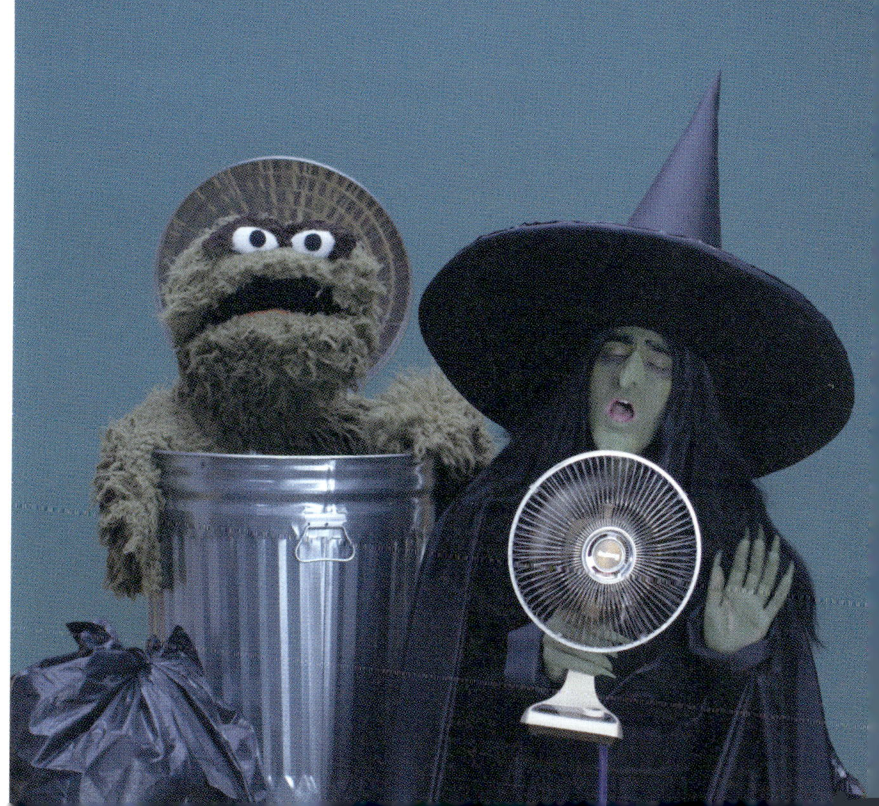

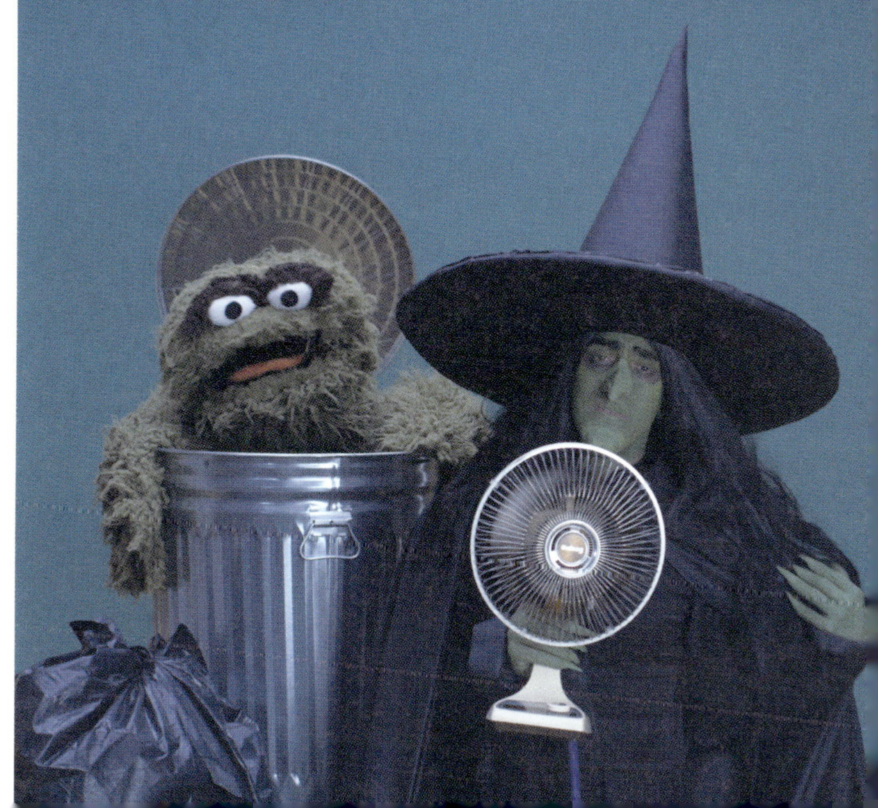

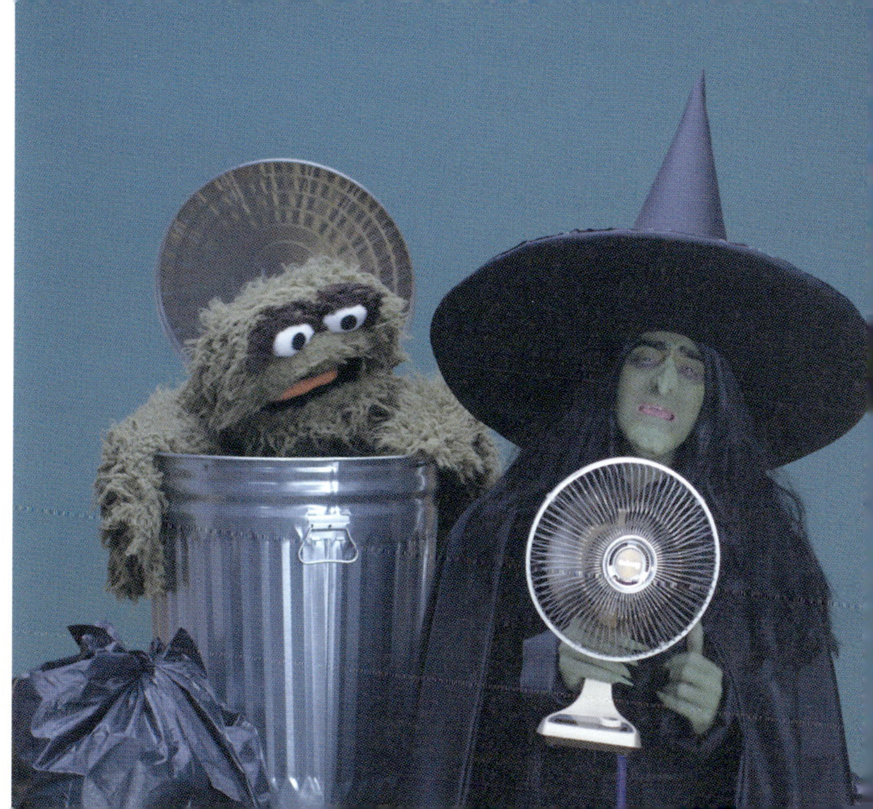

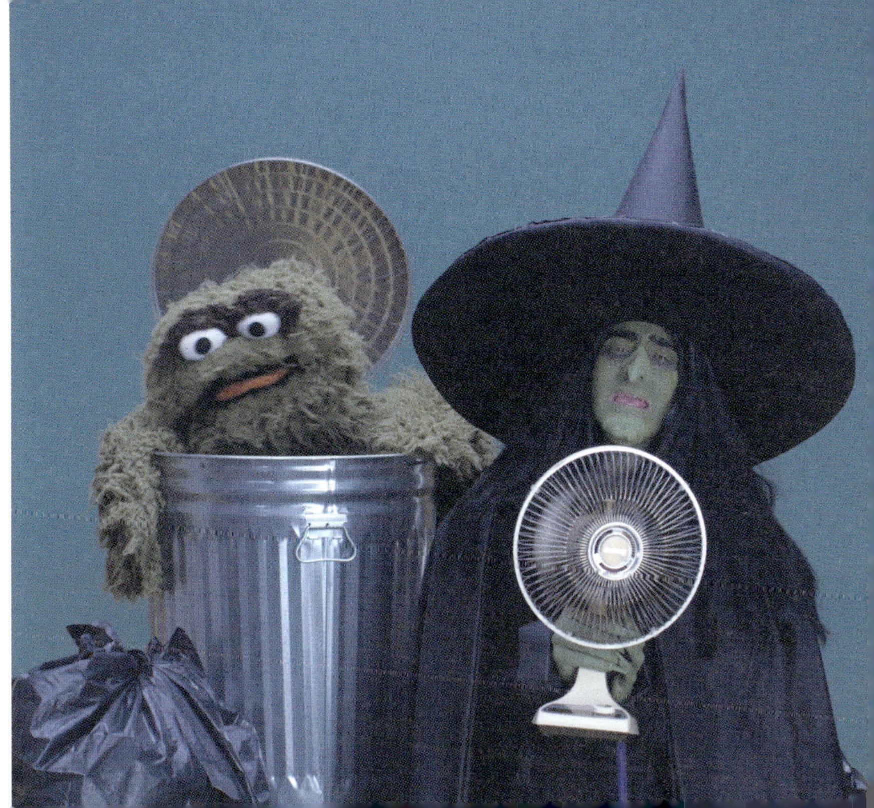

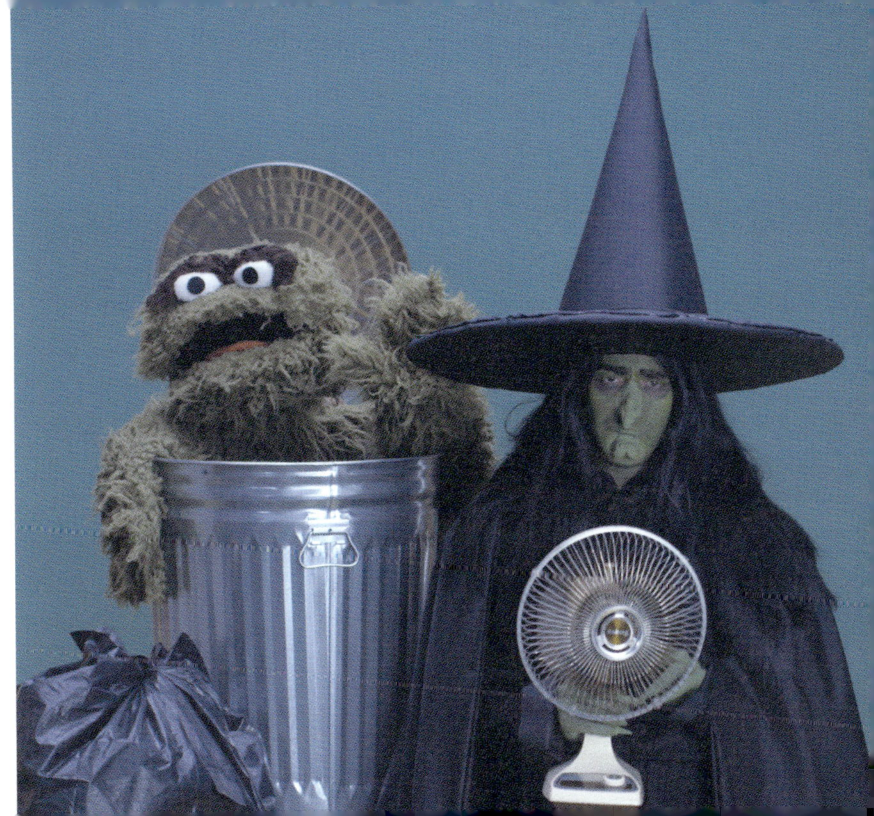

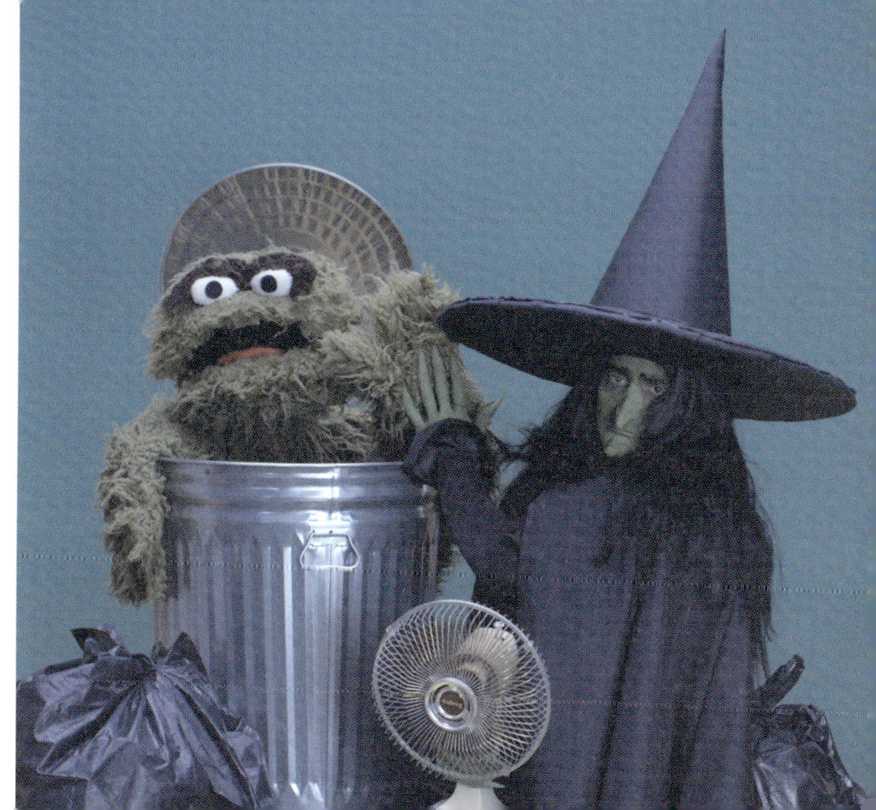

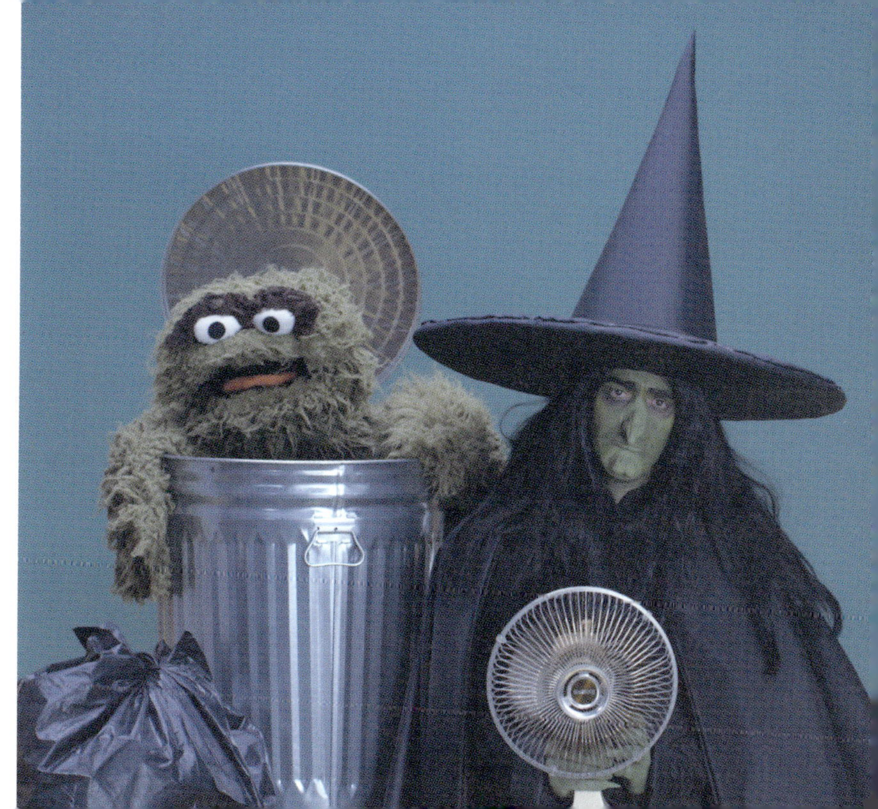

Alex Da Corte *Rubber Pencil Devil*

Published by At Last Books
First printing of 300 copies

Essay by Jamillah James for
A Season in He'll, curated by Jamillah James at Art + Practice,
Los Angeles, in collaboration with the Hammer Museum,
July 9 - September 16, 2016.

Rubber Pencil Devil
HD digital video
TRT: 2:55:52
Edition of 5 + 2AP
Excerpt: 01:59:24 - 02:02:11

ISBN: 978-87-972616-4-4

Thank you Margaret, Carroll, Jamillah, Anna and all of the witches.

Rubber Pencil Devil is a series of 57 flipbooks compiling unrecorded, unpublished and ephemeral texts by, with and about Alex Da Corte.